MOVE IT!
STUDENTS' BOOK

3

FIONA BEDDALL AND JAYNE WILDMAN
SERIES CONSULTANT: CARA NORRIS-RAMIREZ

Unit	Page	Grammar	Vocabulary
Starter Unit	4	Be/Have; Is/'s; Pronouns and possessive 's; Possessive adjectives, Indefinite pronouns; Present simple; Adverbs of frequency; Was/Were	Common verbs; Prepositions; Everyday objects; School subjects; Numbers and dates; Opinion adjectives
1 Home Sweet Home ❑ Geography File	10	Present simple and continuous Verb + -ing	Rooms and parts of the house Furniture and household objects
2 What's the Story? ❑ Real World Profiles	20	Past simple; Past continuous Past simple vs Past continuous	Adjectives to describe pictures Adjective + preposition
3 It's a Bargain! ❑ Math File	30	Comparatives and superlatives Too and enough Much, many, a lot of	Shopping nouns Money verbs
Review 1 Units 1–3	40		
4 In the News ❑ Real World Profiles	44	Present perfect Present perfect vs Past simple	News and media Adverbs of manner
5 Enjoy Your Vacation! ❑ Literature File	54	Present perfect + for and since; How long? Past simple with just	Vacation Meanings of get
6 That's Life! ❑ Real World Profiles	64	Have to/Don't have to; Must/Mustn't Predictions with will, won't, might	Household chores Feelings adjectives
Review 2 Units 4–6	74		
7 Make a Difference ❑ Global Citizenship File	78	Be going to and will First conditional	Protest and support Verb + preposition
8 Danger and Risk ❑ Real World Profiles	88	Second conditional Relative pronouns	Extreme adjectives Illness and injury
9 Inventions ❑ Science File	98	Present simple passive Past simple passive	Machine nouns and verbs Word building
Review 3 Units 7–9	108		
Brain Trainers	112		
Listening Bank	118		
Culture	121		
Irregular Verb List	127		

Reading and Listening	Speaking and Pronunciation	Writing
School Intranet	Asking for and giving personal information	A personal profile
Live Small What Does Your Bedroom Say About You? 🎧 Hannah's bedroom 🎧 Dictation	Describing a place **Pronunciation:** /v/, /w/ and /b/	A description of a room **Writing File:** Linking words: addition and contrast
Click! Magazine: Young Photographer Contest Great Moments in History 🎧 Talking about a photo 🎧 Dictation	Permission **Pronunciation:** Sentence stress	A description of a picture **Writing File:** Describing a picture
Boston Market Wins More Customers The Internet—the World's Biggest Market 🎧 Problems with buying things online 🎧 Dictation	Asking for help **Pronunciation:** /ɔ/ and /oʊ/	A customer review **Writing File:** Expressing opinion
Survey: Teens and the Media Profile: Christiane Amanpour 🎧 Opinions about the news 🎧 Dictation	Doubt and disbelief **Pronunciation:** /æ/ and /ɑ/	A profile **Writing File:** Error correction
Behind the Camera Strange Tourist Attractions 🎧 Radio interview 🎧 Dictation	Asking for information **Pronunciation:** /aɪ/ vs /ɪ/	A travel guide **Writing File:** Making your writing more interesting
Today's Teens Don't Do Chores Future Teens 🎧 Teenagers of the future 🎧 Dictation	Giving advice **Pronunciation:** /ʌ/ and /yu/	A problem page **Writing File:** Linking words: reason and result
Dana Point Elephant Parade Do Something Different … 🎧 An interview about a charity 🎧 Dictation	Persuading **Pronunciation:** *going to*	A formal letter **Writing File:** Letter writing
Interview: Naomi Daniels Why Are People Risk-Takers? 🎧 Talking about a TV show 🎧 Dictation	Talking about health **Pronunciation:** *gh*	An application form **Writing File:** Completing an application form
Teenage Inventors A Book for All Time? 🎧 Reading stories on a smart phone 🎧 Dictation	Problems with machines **Pronunciation:** /ɪ/ and /i/	An opinion essay **Writing File:** How to write an opinion essay

Contents 3

Starter Unit

Grammar and Vocabulary • To be

1 Complete the sentences with the correct form of *to be*.

1 My brother *is* only ten, so he …. (not) at my school.
2 They …. (not) at home. Where …. (they)?
3 " …. (we) late for school?" "Yes, you …. ."
4 I …. (not) British. I …. American.
5 " …. there a mall in this town?" "Yes, there …. , but there …. (not) any good stores in it."

• Have

2 Choose the correct options.

1 I *have / has* a new pen.
2 *Does she have / She has* any brothers or sisters?
3 *He have / He has* some difficult homework tonight.
4 The movie doesn't *have / has* any good actors in it.
5 Do you *have / has* time for a coffee?
6 We *doesn't have / don't have* a dog.

• Be and have

3 Look at the picture and complete the sentences. Use the correct form of *be* or *have*, positive or negative.

1 He *doesn't have* blond hair.
2 She …. beautiful.
3 They …. curly hair.
4 He …. big.
5 He …. long hair.
6 She …. brown eyes.
7 He …. handsome.
8 She …. thin.

• Possessive 's

4 Complete the sentences with *'s* or *s'*.

1 She's *William's* (William) sister.
2 Those are my …. (friend) shoes.
3 The …. (dogs) legs are very short.
4 I can't see over the …. (people) heads.
5 The …. (man) hat is on the chair.
6 Look at those …. (girls) hairstyles!

• *Is* and possessive *'s*

5 Look at the *'s* in these sentences. Is it *is* or possessive?

1 The student's name is Hannah. *possessive*
2 He's in London.
3 Katie's good with computers.
4 The book's under the bed.
5 The book's pages are dirty.
6 Dan's mom has a new job.

• Subject and object pronouns

6 Choose the correct words.

1 She likes Matt, but *she / her* doesn't like James.
2 You can visit *they / them* tomorrow.
3 Please listen to *I / me*.
4 *He / Him* has a new car.
5 My grandparents don't live with *we / us*.
6 I want to help *she / her*.
7 Why do *they / them* like golf? It's boring!
8 When my brother plays football, we watch *he / him*.

• Possessive adjectives

7 Rewrite the sentences. Use possessive adjectives.

1 I have a very old computer.
   My computer is very old.
2 It has a small screen.
3 You have nice parents.
4 They have red hair.
5 He has a new T-shirt.
6 We have difficult homework.

4 Starter Unit

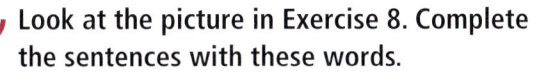

• Common verbs

8 Match the verbs (1–8) to the activities in the picture (a–h).

1 fly *b*
2 eat
3 play
4 run
5 sail
6 climb
7 jump
8 swim

• Prepositions

9 Look at the picture in Exercise 8. Complete the sentences with these words.

around	behind	in front of	into	next to
~~on~~	over	under	up	

1 There's a tower *on* the island.
2 Someone is sailing …. the island.
3 A plane is flying …. the beach.
4 The sun is …. a cloud.
5 A girl is sitting …. the tent.
6 There's a CD player …. the girl.
7 A boy is climbing …. a tree.
8 His friend is jumping …. the ocean.
9 A ball is …. a chair.

• Indefinite pronouns

10 Complete the conversation with these words.

anything	~~everyone~~	everything
no one	someone	something

A Where is ¹ *everyone* today?
B They're all at the beach.
A Oh right! ² …. invited me, too. Who was it? Kate, I think.
B You're lucky. ³ …. invited me.
A Oh, I'm sorry.
B I don't mind. I don't like swimming, and I don't have ⁴ …. to wear at the beach.
A Come and buy ⁵ …. new at the store now! What about a new T-shirt?
B No. ⁶ …. in the store right now is expensive, and I don't have any money.

• Everyday objects

11 Match the beginnings of the words to the endings. Then match the words to the pictures.

1 maga	book
2 cam	et
3 lap	ter
4 wall	ns
5 note	zine *picture e*
6 pos	top
7 wa	era
8 swea	ter
9 jea	tch

• School subjects

12 Complete the words (1–8). Then match them to the pictures (a–h).

1 s c i *e n c* e   *picture c*
2 m a _ _
3 h _ _ _ _ r y
4 g e o g _ _ _ _ _
5 E _ _ l i _ _
6 m u s _ _
7 a _ _
8 l _ t _ _ _ t _ _ _

• Present simple: affirmative and negative

13 Complete the sentences with the correct form of the verbs.

1 She *doesn't live* (not live) here.
2 They .... (not eat) vegetables.
3 He .... (fly) to the Caribbean every summer.
4 She .... (watch) TV in the evening.
5 We .... (get up) at seven o'clock.
6 It .... (not work).
7 You .... (not know) Liam.
8 I .... (take) a shower every day.

Starter Unit

- ## Present simple: questions and short answers

14 Complete the questions and then answer them.

1 *Do you like* (you/like) science? ✓ *Yes, I do.*
2 .... (Jessica/learn) English? ✗
3 .... (we/do) PE on Tuesdays? ✗
4 .... (they/study) math on the weekend? ✓
5 .... (I/need) a new geography book? ✗
6 .... (he/teach) history? ✓

- ## Adverbs of frequency

15 Write these words in the sequence.

| always | hardly ever | ~~never~~ |
| often | sometimes | usually |

0%
1 *never*
2 ....
3 ....
4 ....
5 ....
100%
6 ....

16 Make true sentences. Use adverbs of frequency.

1 I / late / for school
  I am sometimes late for school.
2 My class / listen / to the teacher
3 We / do / our homework
4 Our classes / interesting
5 I / take / the bus / to school
6 My friends / walk / home from school / with me

- ## Numbers and dates

17 What are the missing numbers and words?

1 13 *thirteen*
2 .... seven hundred and twenty-two
3 490 ....
4 .... six thousand, one hundred and ten
5 3,412 ....
6 .... eight million

18 How do we say these dates?

1 Jan 1 *January first*   5 Nov 8
2 Aug 3   6 Apr 25
3 Mar 14   7 Dec 23
4 Sept 2   8 Oct 31

- ## Was/Were

19 Complete the conversation with the correct form of *was* or *were*.

A When were you born?
B I [1] *was* born on July 2, 1997. But I [2] .... (not) born in this country. My parents [3] .... in Kenya.
A Why [4] .... they there?
B My mom [5] .... a nurse there, and my dad [6] .... an engineer.
A [7] .... they happy in Kenya?
B Yes, they [8] .... , but there [9] .... (not) any good schools near our home in Kenya. That's why we live here now.

- ## Opinion adjectives

20 Complete the adjectives in these sentences.

1 A lot of classical music is very r o m a n t i c.
2 Science fiction movies are very ex _ _ t _ _ g.
3 Mexican food is very t _ s _ y.
4 A lot of animations are very f _ _ n _ .
5 Rap music is t _ rr _ bl _.
6 This is an _ w _ s _ m _ football game!
7 Museums are b _ r _ _ g.
8 Skiing is e _ p _ _ s _ v _ .
9 Rock climbing is sc _ r _ .
10 A tarantula is a w _ _ rd pet!
11 A lot of children's TV shows are _ n _ oy _ _ g.

21 Give your opinion. Make six sentences, using adjectives from Exercise 20 and some of these words.

action movies	bowling	documentaries
fish	horror movies	jazz
judo	musicals	opera
pasta	rock music	skateboarding
surfing	vegetables	

Skateboarding is an exciting sport.

Speaking and Listening

1 Read and listen to the conversation. Correct the answers.

Ruby
1 Where are you from?
   I'm from ~~Miami~~. *Orlando*
2 Why do you live in Frederick now?
   Because my dad has a new job here.
3 When did you move to Frederick?
   Yesterday.
4 How old are you?
   I'm seventeen.

Tom
5 Who do you have in your family?
   My mom, my dad and my sister Ruby.
6 Which road does your family live on?
   Ash Road.
7 How do you go to school?
   I go by bike.
8 When do you leave in the morning?
   At eight o'clock.

2 Act out the conversation in groups of four.

Ruby Excuse me, where's room 27?
Ella It's on the left here. We can show you.
Ruby Thanks.
Ash Are you new at this school?
Ruby Yes. I only moved here last week.
Ash Welcome to Frederick! Where are you from?
Ruby Orlando, but my mom has a job here now.
Tom Where do you live?
Ruby On Talbot Road.
Ella We live there, too—at number 72 Talbot Road. What about you?
Ruby Our house is number 73!
Tom Cool! We can see your house from our window. I'm Tom. This is my sister, Ella, and this is our friend, Ash. We're all fourteen.
Ruby Me, too! Hi, guys. I'm Ruby.
Ella Hey, do you want to walk to school with us tomorrow? We usually leave at eight fifteen.
Ruby Sure! Thanks.

3 Complete the sentences from the conversation.
1 *Welcome* to Frederick!
2 What .... you?
3 I'm Tom. .... is my sister, Ella.
4 Hi, ... I'm Ruby.

Reading

4 Read the page from the school website.

Year 10

Hi! My name's Ash Simmons. I'm fourteen years old and I live with my mom and my big sister, Samina. My favorite things are my computer games and my blue baseball cap. I listen to a lot of music, usually hip hop or rap, and I love skateboarding.

My name's Tom Green and I'm fourteen. I like football and computer games. I play the guitar, too. It's fun, but I'm not very good! My perfect day is a lazy day in the sun with my friends. Oh, and I love science fiction movies. My favorite movie is *The Matrix*.

Hi! I'm Ella Green and I'm fourteen. I like romantic movies, celebrity magazines and new friends. My favorite thing? My pink top … or my new red shoes … or my California T-shirt … oh, I can't choose!

My name's Ruby Madding and I'm fourteen. My favorite hobby is surfing, but I also like climbing and skateboarding. I love hot weather—it's hot in Orlando right now. I usually listen to rock music. My favorite band is Black River Drive.

5 Read the website again. Copy and complete the table.

Name	Ash ….
Likes	computer games, …. , …. and rap music, ….
Name	…. Green
Likes	…. movies, …. magazines, new …. , clothes
Name	Tom ….
Likes	…. , computer games, the …. , …. movies
Name	Ruby Madding
Likes	…. , climbing, …. , …. weather, …. music

Writing

6 Make your profile for the school website.

 My assessment profile: Workbook page 126

1 Home Sweet Home

Grammar
Present simple and continuous; Verb + -ing

Vocabulary
Rooms and parts of the house; Furniture and household objects

Speaking
Describing a place

Writing
A description of a room

Word list page 43
Workbook page 104

Vocabulary • Rooms and parts of the house

1 Match the pictures of the parts of the house (1–16) to these words.
1.3 Then listen, check and repeat.

attic	balcony
basement	ceiling
driveway	fireplace
floor	garage
hallway	landing
office	patio 1
roof	stairs
wall	yard

2 Complete the sentences with the words in Exercise 1.

1 The *stairs* go up to the bedrooms at the top of a house.
2 You come into the house through the _ _ _ _ _ _ _ .
3 There's a bird on the _ _ _ _ .
4 The _ _ _ _ _ _ is next to the bathroom.
5 The red car is inside the _ _ _ _ _ _ .
6 There are boxes of old toys in the _ _ _ _ _ .
7 It's warm near the _ _ _ _ _ _ _ _ _ in the living room.
8 Someone is mowing the lawn in the _ _ _ _ .

3 Tell a partner about your home.

1 Do you live in a house or an apartment?
2 Describe the outside of your house or apartment.
  • Is it big or small?
  • What color are the walls and roof?
  • Is there a balcony, a yard, a garage, a driveway?
3 Describe the inside of your house or apartment.
  • Is there a hallway, an attic, a basement, an office?
  • What color are the walls, floor and ceiling in your bedroom and your living room?

> Our house is small. It has white walls and a red roof. There's a yard with a small patio. There's a driveway, but there isn't a garage.

**Brain Trainer Unit 1
Activity 2**
Go to page 112

Reading

1 Look at the photo. What do you think this building is for?

2 Read the text quickly. Choose the best answer.
1 Austin is a *teenager* / *adult*.
2 The building is *his bedroom* / *a complete house*.
3 He wants to *live in it* / *sell it*.

3 Read the text again. Answer the questions.
1 How are families in Europe and North America changing?
   The size of an average family is getting smaller.
2 What are the disadvantages of big homes?
3 Where is Austin's bedroom?
4 What is 3.7 meters long?
5 What does Austin like about his house?
6 What happens when a building job is difficult for Austin?
7 Does Austin live in his house all the time? Why?/Why not?
8 Why is his house useful for the future?

4 In pairs, ask and answer.
1 Are many homes in your country bigger than they need to be?
2 Imagine your family in a house that is half the size of your home now. How is your life different? What is better? What is worse?
3 Would you like to live on your own in a house like Austin's? Why?/Why not?

Tumbleweed Tiny House company

Live Small

In Europe and North America, the size of an average family is getting smaller, but homes are not. In many countries they are getting bigger. Bigger homes are more expensive, and heating them in cold weather is worse for the environment. Many people believe it's time to think again about the size of our homes. Sixteen-year-old Austin Hay is building a home on his parents' driveway. It has everything important, including a bathroom, a kitchen and an attic bedroom with a low ceiling, but it's only 2.4 meters wide and 3.7 meters long.

"When I was a kid, I wanted to build a tree house," Austin explains. "But this house is on wheels, and that's a lot cooler."

Austin doesn't do any building during the week—he's busy with homework and playing baseball. But he usually works hard on his house on the weekend. "Right now I'm working on the doors. They're really easy, so my dad isn't helping me. He only helps with the difficult things."

Austin is sleeping in his little house this summer. There isn't a fireplace yet, so in the winter he'll move back across the yard to his parents' house. And in the future? "College is very expensive in the US, but it'll be cheaper for me because I can take my little house with me. I can live in it anywhere."

Unit 1 • Home Sweet Home

Grammar • Present simple and continuous

Present simple	Present continuous
He always makes good food.	He is making dinner at the moment.
I live with my dad.	They're staying in a house without any adults.

Grammar reference Workbook page 86

1 Study the grammar table. Match the sentence beginnings (1–2) to the endings (a–d) to complete the rules.

1 We use the Present simple …
2 We use the Present continuous …
  a for routines and habits.
  b for actions in progress.
  c for temporary situations.
  d for permanent situations and general truths.

2 Choose the correct options.

1 Kat *doesn't talk / isn't talking* to me today.
2 I *always go / am always going* to bed at nine o'clock.
3 We *often go / are often going* to the movies on the weekend.
4 *I'm learning / I learn* about electricity in science this week.

3 Complete the phone conversation with the Present continuous form of the verbs.

A Hi, Ellie. How are you?
B Fine, thanks, Grandma.
A How ¹ *are you feeling* (you/feel) about your exams?
B Not too bad, thanks. I ² …. (study) on the balcony right now.
A ³ …. (the sun/shine) there?
B Yes, it ⁴ …. (shine). It's really nice out!
A You're lucky! Your grandpa and I ⁵ …. (wear) our coats in the house because it's so cold! What ⁶ …. (Callum and Leo/do)?
B They ⁷ …. (listen) to music in the basement. Do you want to talk to them?
A Actually, I want to talk to your dad.
B OK. He ⁸ …. (wash) the car in the driveway. Wait a minute …

4 Complete the text with the Present simple or Present continuous form of the verbs.

I usually ¹ *take* (take) a bath before bed, but tonight I ² …. (wait) on the landing. Why? Because my brothers Mick and Todd ³ …. (use) the bathroom for band practice. Most people ⁴ …. (not wear) their clothes in the bathtub, but Todd is different. At the moment he ⁵ …. (lie) in the bathtub with all his clothes on. Mick ⁶ …. (sit) on the side of the bathtub, and he ⁷ …. (play) something on the guitar. They usually ⁸ …. (practice) their band music in the garage, but my mom ⁹ …. (paint) flowers on her car in there tonight! I ¹⁰ …. (live) with the world's craziest family!

5 Make questions.

1 you / always / take / a shower or bath / before bed?
   Do you always take a shower or bath before bed?
2 what time / you / usually / go to bed?
3 you / often / get up / late / on the weekend?
4 you / listen / to music / right now?
5 where / you / usually / do / your homework?
6 you / work / hard / right now?

6 What about you? In pairs, ask and answer the questions in Exercise 5.

> Do you always take a shower or bath before bed?

> No. I usually take a shower in the morning.

Unit 1 • Home Sweet Home

Vocabulary • Furniture and household objects

1 Match the pictures (1–13) to these words.
1.5 Then listen, check and repeat.

alarm clock	armchair	blind	bookcase
closet 1	comforter	curtains	cushions
dresser	mirror	pillow	rug
vase			

Word list page 43
Workbook page 104

2 Read the descriptions. Say the thing or things.
1 You put clothes in this. (two things)
   a closet and a dresser
2 You can see your face in this.
3 You put flowers in this.
4 This wakes you up in the morning.
5 You put books in this.
6 This is on the floor. You can walk on it.
7 You sit in this.
8 This keeps you warm in bed.
9 You put your head on this in bed.
10 You put these on your bed or on a chair.

3 Which things from Exercise 1 are in your home? Make sentences.

There's a bookcase in the hallway, next to the living room door.

Pronunciation /v/, /w/ and /b/

4a Listen and repeat.
1.6

| balcony | bookcase | driveway |
| vase | wall | window |

b Listen and repeat. Then practice saying
1.7 the sentences.
1 My favorite vase in the living room is very heavy.
2 Why did you wash the windows and walls?
3 There are blue blinds in my bedroom.
4 I love black-and-white vases.
5 Do you want to have strawberry waffles for breakfast?

5 Say a sentence about the picture in Exercise 1. Your partner says *True* or *False*.

> There's a blue rug on the floor.

> False! There's a green rug on the floor.

**Brain Trainer Unit 1
Activity 3**
Go to page 112

Unit 1 • Home Sweet Home   13

Chatroom Describing a place

Speaking and Listening

1 Look at the photo. Whose house do you think this is?

2 Listen and read the conversation.
1.8 Check your answer.

3 Listen and read again. Choose the correct options.
1.8
1 Ruby *wants / doesn't want* to move again soon.
2 Ash *likes / doesn't like* Ruby's new house.
3 Ruby's bedroom is *big / small*.
4 There's a computer in *Ruby's bedroom / the office*.
5 Ash *wants / doesn't want* to go into the living room.
6 Ella *likes / doesn't like* the town.

4 Act out the conversation in groups of four.

Ruby	Thanks for carrying these boxes in from the driveway, guys.
Tom	No problem! We don't mind helping.
Ruby	I can't stand moving. I never want to see another cardboard box again!
Ash	Your new house is really cool.
Ruby	Thanks, Ash.
Ella	What's your bedroom like?
Ruby	It's a little small, but that's OK. There's space for a dresser and a little desk for my computer. Anyway, I prefer spending time in the yard.
Ella	What's behind that door?
Ruby	The living room. It has a big door out to the patio.
Ash	Let's go out there now. It's a beautiful day.
Tom	Hang on! Let's show Ruby the town first.
Ruby	That would be great. What's the town like?
Ella	It isn't very big, but it's pretty lively.
Ash	Come on, then. Let's go!

Say it in your language …
guys
No problem!
That would be great.
Come on, then.

Unit 1 • Home Sweet Home

5 Look back at the conversation. Find these expressions.

1 a question asking about Ruby's bedroom
   What's your bedroom like? (Ella)
2 an expression describing Ruby's bedroom
3 a question asking about the town
4 two expressions describing the town

6 Read the phrases for describing a place.

Describing a place		
What's it like?		
It's	a little pretty very really	small.

7 Listen to the conversations. Act out the conversations in pairs.
1.9

Ruby   What's ¹ your bedroom like?
Ella   It has ² pretty red walls and a white closet.
Ruby   Is it ³ very big?
Ella   Yes, it is.
Ruby   What's ⁴ the swimming pool like?
Ash   It's very nice. It's ⁵ pretty cold, but it has
       ⁶ a great café.

8 Work in pairs. Replace the words in purple in Exercise 7. Use these words and/or your own ideas. Act out the conversations.

> What's your yard like?

> It has grass and a lot of flowers.

1 your kitchen / your living room / your bathroom
2 green walls and a stove / white walls and a big sofa / pink walls and a large bathtub
3 a little small / very big / really small
4 the park / the library / the shopping mall
5 pretty small / very quiet / really busy
6 a lake / a lot of interesting books / some boring stores

Grammar • Verb + *-ing*

I prefer spending time in the yard.
Tom, Ash and Ella don't mind helping Ruby.
Ruby can't stand moving.
Do you like living here?

Grammar reference Workbook page 86

1 Study the grammar table. Complete the rule.

After the verbs *like, love, hate, enjoy, don't mind,* ....
and ...., we use verb + *-ing*.

2 Complete the sentences with the correct form of these verbs.

do   get   ~~listen~~   sleep   swim   wait

1 I can't stand *listening* to rap music.
2 She hates beds. She prefers .... on the floor.
3 They love .... in the ocean.
4 We don't mind .... our homework.
5 Do you prefer .... up late in the morning?
6 I don't enjoy .... for buses in the rain.

3 Complete the second sentence so it has a similar meaning to the first one. Use the correct form of the word(s) in parentheses and one other word.

1 I think skateboarding is OK. (mind)
   I *don't mind* skateboarding.
2 She never wants to have breakfast. (not like)
   She .... having breakfast.
3 He's very happy when he rides his bike. (love)
   He .... his bike.
4 It's better when we have band practice in the basement. (prefer)
   We .... band practice in the basement.
5 They hate doing homework. (not stand)
   They .... doing homework.

4 Make three questions with *Do you like* + *-ing*. Then ask and answer in pairs.

> Do you like going to the beach?

> Yes, I love it. What about you?

> I don't mind it, but I prefer going to a swimming pool.

Unit 1 • Home Sweet Home

Reading

1 Read the magazine article quickly. Choose the best heading.

1 Clean Up Your Room!
2 What Does Your Bedroom Say About You?
3 How to Have a Cool Bedroom

You can't always choose your room, but you can choose the things inside it. Because of that, your bedroom says a lot about your personality.

And we're not only talking about your favorite hobbies or your taste in music and books. Of course, a guitar behind the door or sci-fi stories in your bookcase give people information about you, but a careful look at your bedroom can teach them a lot more than that.

The colors in your room, for example, are very interesting. Does your room have bright colors on the walls, curtains, a rug or a comforter? Then you probably love trying new things. People with pale walls are often friendly and talkative, but people with dark walls don't like meeting new people. Black and white is a popular choice for people with strong opinions.

How big is your closet? A big closet often means that you are into fashion, but not always. It can also be a sign that you hate throwing old things away and prefer keeping everything behind your closet door. Someone with a neat room is usually cheerful, but someone with a messy room is moodier and often unhappy. The pictures on your walls say a lot, too. Generous people like decorating their rooms with photos of their friends and family, but if your own face is in every picture or you have more than one mirror, watch out! This shows that you are probably a little selfish.

So, before you invite your friends into your bedroom, think carefully. What message will your bedroom give them about you?

Key Words
taste   careful   bright
pale   decorate   watch out

2 Read the article again. Answer the questions.

1.10
1 What two things give information about your tastes and interests?
The colors in your room and the pictures on the walls.
2 What type of colors do shy people often have on their walls?
3 Why do people have big closets? Find two reasons in the article.
4 You are usually smiling. What does the article say about your room?
5 You like buying presents for people. What do you probably have on your walls?
6 What two things show that a person thinks only about himself/herself?

Listening

1 Hannah is talking to a friend about her
1.11 bedroom and the article above. Listen and answer the questions.

1 What does Hannah's bedroom say about her?
2 Why does she want to buy a lock for her door?

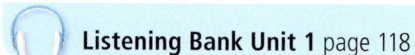
Listening Bank Unit 1 page 118

2 In pairs, ask and answer. Is the article right about you?

1 Do you have any bright colors in your bedroom?
2 Are there any pictures of your friends on the walls?
3 Are there any pictures of you?
4 How many mirrors are there?
5 Is your room neat?

Writing • A description of a room

1 Read the Writing File.

> **Writing File** Linking words: addition and contrast
>
> **You can link similar ideas with *and*, *also* and *too*.**
>   You're really talkative, and you like trying new things.
>   The rug is green. The comforter is also green.
>   The colors are interesting. The pictures are interesting, too.
>
> **You can link contrasting ideas with *but* and *however*.**
>   I have some pictures of friends, but I don't have any pictures of myself.
>   I love red. However, I don't like the bright red walls in my living room.

2 Read about Matt's favorite room. Find the linking words.

My Favorite Room
by Matt Davies

My favorite room is the office at home. It's a little small, but it's really light, and it's always very quiet. There's a big desk under the window. On the desk there's a computer and a lamp. There's a box of pens and pencils, too. In front of the desk there's a chair with green cushions. The walls are white, and there's a blue and green blind on the window. The carpet in the office is also blue and green.
I love sitting at the desk and watching all the people in the street. I usually do my homework in this room. However, when I don't have any homework, I like playing games on the computer.

3 Complete the sentences with *and*, *also*, *too*, *but* and *however*.

1 He has a big closet for his clothes *and* he has two big dressers.
2 My alarm clock wakes me up in the morning, and it can play the radio, ...
3 We watch TV in the kitchen, and we .... do our homework there.
4 I like playing tennis. ...., I don't play very often.
5 I have three pet lizards in my bedroom, and I .... have a pet snake.
6 There's a pillow on the bed, ... there isn't a comforter.

4 Read Matt's description again. Answer the questions.

1 What room is it? *The office*
2 What adjectives does he use to describe it?
3 What furniture is there in the room?
4 What color are the walls?
5 Are there other things in the room of a different color?
6 What does he like doing in the room?

5 Think about your favorite room. Use the questions in Exercise 4 to help you. Take notes.

6 Write a description of your favorite room. Use "My favorite room" and your notes from Exercise 5.

> **My favorite room**
>
> **Paragraph 1**
> Introduce the room and give a general description.
> *My favorite room is .... . There's a .... .*
>
> **Paragraph 2**
> Describe the furniture and walls.
> *The walls are .... and .... .*
>
> **Paragraph 3**
> Say what you like doing in the room.
> *I like .... .*

> **Remember!**
> • Use linking words *and*, *also*, *too*, *but*, *however*.
> • Use the vocabulary in this unit.
> • Check your grammar, spelling and punctuation.

Unit 1 • Home Sweet Home

Refresh Your Memory!

Grammar • Review

1 Complete the conversation with the correct form of the verbs.

A What ¹ *are you reading* (you/read)?
B A postcard from my dad. He ² …. (work) in Montreal at the moment, so we only ³ …. (see) him on weekends.
A ⁴ …. (he/like) Montreal?
B Yes, he loves it. He ⁵ …. (look) for a new home for us there, but my mom doesn't want to go. All our friends and family ⁶ …. (live) here in the US, and she ⁷ …. (not speak) any French.
A ⁸ …. (you/speak) French?
B Well, we ⁹ …. (have) French classes every day at school, but people in Quebec always ¹⁰ …. (talk) really fast. I ¹¹ …. (not understand) very much!

2 Complete the sentences with the correct form of these verbs.

~~cook~~	eat	go	learn	live
not do	not listen	play	visit	watch

1 My dad usually *cooks* our dinner, but tonight we …. in a restaurant.
2 We …. about China in geography class right now. 1.3 billion people …. in China!
3 They …. to their new CD. They …. a movie.
4 She …. judo on Thursdays. She …. volleyball.
5 I …. to school in Connecticut, but today we …. a museum in New York.

3 Make sentences and questions.

1 he / love / play / basketball
   He loves playing basketball.
2 you / enjoy / run?
3 she / not mind / go / by bus
4 you / hate / lose
5 I / not like / learn / French
6 he / prefer / study / computer science?
7 they / can't stand / listen / to rap music

Vocabulary • Review

4 Complete the sentences with the correct rooms and parts of the house.

1 Come and have a drink on the *patio*. It's sunny today.
2 The light on the l _ _ _ _ _ _ outside my bedroom doesn't work.
3 The dog usually sleeps under the table in the h _ _ _ _ _ _ .
4 The c _ _ _ _ _ _ in the attic is very low. I can't stand up in there.
5 There's a big mirror above the f _ _ _ _ _ _ _ _ .
6 The grass in the y _ _ _ looks a little dry.

5 Match the beginnings (1–5) to the endings (a–e) of the sentences.

1 There are flowers in the   *e*
2 On the floor there's a
3 He went to bed and put his head on the
4 She loves looking at herself in the
5 That window needs a

a pillow.
b mirror.
c blind.
d rug.
e vase.

Speaking • Review

6 Put the conversation in the correct order (1–6).
1.12 Then listen and check.

a Do you spend any time there?
b It's a little small, and it isn't very sunny.
c It's very nice. It has really big windows and some very comfortable armchairs.
d What's your balcony like? *1*
e No, I don't. I prefer hanging out in the living room.
f What's that like?

Dictation

7 Listen and write in your notebook.
1.13

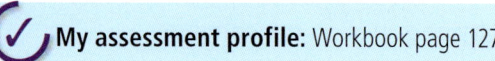

My assessment profile: Workbook page 127

18 Unit 1 • Home Sweet Home

Geography File

Houses Around the World

1. Mongolia is near Russia and China in northeast Asia. The winters in Mongolia are very long and very cold. Many Mongolians keep horses. They move from place to place two or three times a year so their animals have enough food. When they move, their homes go with them. Their homes are called yurts, and they must be strong because there are often winds of 160 km an hour.

2. The city of Hong Kong, in the south of China, is located on a peninsula and two small islands. There are many mountains in Hong Kong, so there isn't a lot of space for houses. The buildings are very tall to save space. There are more tall buildings here than in any other city in the world. Forty percent of the people live higher than the fourteenth floor! Most people live in really small apartments, but they don't mind. They often eat in restaurants, and they don't spend a lot of time at home.

3. Belize is a small country in Central America. It is hot year round, with a wet and a dry season. A lot of people live in stilt houses near the ocean. This type of house stays cool because the wind blows through it. It is also protected from snakes and other animals because it is not on the ground. People often leave their car under the house, out of the hot sun. From June to November, there are sometimes terrible storms, but the ocean water doesn't come into the house.

Key Words
peninsula   space   stilt
blow   ground

Reading

1 Read about these homes. Match the photos (a–c) to the paragraphs (1–3).
1.14

2 Listen to a description of another home. Choose the correct words to complete the fact file.
1.15

My Geography File

3 In groups, make a fact file about a home in another part of the world. Use the questions in Exercise 2 to help you.

4 Prepare a presentation for the class, including pictures or photos if possible. Then give your presentation.

Where is it?
Swiss [1] *mountains* / *valleys*

What is the climate like?
[2] *warm* / *windy* in summer [3] *snowy* / *rainy* in winter

What is the home like? Why?
[4] *big* / *small* roof – protects the walls from bad weather
fireplace in the [5] *center* / *back* of the house – keeps people warm
[6] *patio* / *balcony* – people can enjoy the sun in summer

Unit 1 • Home Sweet Home

2 What's the Story?

Grammar
Past simple; Past continuous; Past simple vs Past continuous

Vocabulary
Adjectives to describe pictures; Adjective + preposition

Speaking
Permission

Writing
A description of a picture

Word list page 43
Workbook page 105

Vocabulary • Adjectives to describe pictures

1 Match the photos (1–6) to the comments (a–f). Check the meaning of the words in bold in a dictionary. Then listen, check and repeat.
1.16

a It's an **interesting** photo of a famous place. It's very **dramatic**.
b It's a **boring**, **silly** photo. I don't like it. 1
c I love wildlife photos. This one is **dark**, but it's **beautiful**.
d It's a little **blurry**, but I like it. It's really **colorful**!
e It's obviously **fake**, and it looks really **horrible**!
f The clothes are **old-fashioned**, but the photo is **funny**.

2 Complete the sentences with the adjectives in Exercise 1.

1 My little brother is so *silly*. He's always telling jokes.
2 She often wears .... clothes. Red and green T-shirts are her favorite.
3 My cat moved when I took this photo, so it's .... .
4 It's very .... in here. Can you turn on the light?
5 Everyone said the famous photo was .... . Nobody thought it was real.
6 The storm last night was really .... . The sky was purple! But I hate storms—I think they're .... .

3 In pairs, ask and answer about the photos. Use the adjectives in Exercise 1.

> Do you like photo 1?

> Yes, I do. I think it's .... and .... . What do you think?

> I disagree. I think it's .... .

Brain Trainer Unit 2
Activity 2
Go to page 113

Unit 2 • What's the Story?

Reading

1 Look at the title of the magazine article and the photos. What do you think you are going to read about?

2 Read the article quickly and check your ideas.

3 Match the photos (a–c) to the paragraphs (1–3).

4 Read the article again. Answer the questions.
1. What do the winners get?
   The winners get a digital camera.
2. What is Lucas's photo of?
3. Where was Laine?
4. What is the weather like in Carrie's photo?
5. Does CLICK like Carrie's photo?
6. Does Jared like his photo?
7. Where were Jared and his family?

5 **What about you?** In pairs, ask and answer.
1. Do you take a lot of photos? What do you use—a camera or your cell phone?
2. Did you take any photos on your last vacation? What were they like?
3. Describe the best photo you took last year.

CLICK! Magazine — Young Photographer Contest

Every year at **CLICK!** Magazine, kids from all over the country send in photos for our fantastic contest. Here are this year's winners! The best photo in each category won a digital camera.

❶ People
Photographer: Lucas
Subject: My sister

Lucas says: On August 5 we were driving to Canada for our summer vacation. I took this picture of my sister, Laine, in the back of our car. It was a long drive, and she wasn't enjoying it.
CLICK says: Lucas's photo is interesting and funny. You can see his sister's thoughts in her face. What was she thinking? How was she feeling? This photo really tells a story.

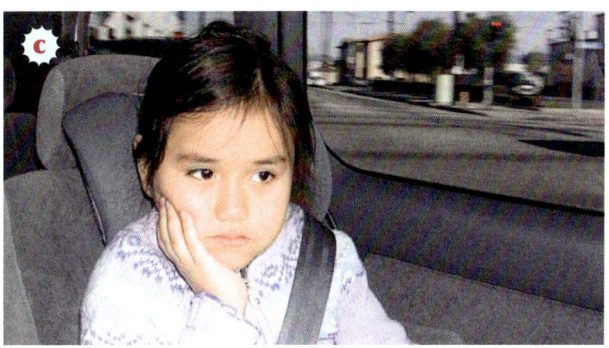

❷ Places
Photographer: Carrie
Subject: A storm

Carrie says: Last month I was on vacation in Scotland with my family. There were a lot of storms, and this was a very windy day! The grass and the trees were moving. The picture is a little blurry, but I like it!
CLICK says: Carrie's picture is very dramatic. When you look at her picture, you can almost feel the wind!

❸ Animals
Photographer: Jared
Subject: On safari

Jared says: Last year I went on vacation to the Serengeti National Park. I was really stupid—I didn't have my camera—but I took a lot of photos with my mom's phone. This one is my favorite. It was 3 o'clock in the afternoon, and it was raining. We weren't driving around—we were waiting for the rain to stop. That's when I saw the elephants.
CLICK says: This is a beautiful photo!

Grammar • Past simple

Last year I went on vacation to the Serengeti National Park.
I didn't have my camera.
I took this picture of my sister, Laine.

Grammar reference Workbook page 88

1 Study the grammar table. Choose the correct option to complete the rule.

The Past simple describes *a finished action / an action in progress* in the past.

We use the Past simple with past time adverbials, e.g., *yesterday, last week/year/Tuesday, two hours/days/weeks ago*

2 Complete the sentences with the Past simple form of these verbs.

| get   not go   not play   see   take   watch |

1 We *saw* the photo yesterday, and we all thought it was fake.
2 They …. on vacation last year. They stayed at home.
3 …. you …. my email?
4 I …. football last weekend. I couldn't because the weather was horrible!
5 She …. a photo and put it on her blog a few minutes ago.
6 "…. you …. the movie last night?"
"Yes, we did. It was really boring!"

3 What about you? In pairs, ask and answer.

1 What did you watch on TV yesterday?
2 Did you do any homework?
3 What did you do last weekend?
4 Did you take any photos of your friends?
5 Where did you go on vacation last year?
6 Did you have a good time?

> What did you watch on TV yesterday?

> I watched the news.

• Past continuous

On August 5 we were driving to Canada.
We weren't driving around.
What was she thinking?

Grammar reference Workbook page 88

4 Study the grammar table. Choose the correct option to complete the rule.

The Past continuous describes *a finished action / an action in progress* in the past.

5 Complete the sentences with the Past continuous form of the verbs.

1 I *was waiting* outside the movie theater at 7 p.m. Luckily it …. . (wait/not rain)
2 At 9 o'clock last night they …. on the phone. They …. their homework. (talk/not do)
3 …. he …. football at 5 o'clock? No, he …. a game on TV. (play/watch)
4 At 8:30 a.m. she …. to school; she …. on a bus. (not bike/sit)
5 What …. you …. on January 1? …. you …. a party? (do/have)
6 At 1 o'clock I …. sandwiches; I …. pasta. (make/not cook)

6 Read about a day in the life of a wildlife photographer. What was happening at different times of the day?

1 9 o'clock / she / cook / breakfast
   At 9 o'clock she was cooking breakfast.
2 11 o'clock / they / look for / animals
3 1 o'clock / they / sit in the jeep
4 3 o'clock / she / take / photographs
5 5 o'clock / they / go back / home
6 7 o'clock / she / read / a book

Unit 2 • What's the Story?

Pronunciation Sentence stress

7a Listen and repeat.
1.18 At 7 o'clock she was reading a book.

b Listen. Which words are stressed?
1.19
1 What were you doing at 8 o'clock?
2 Were you watching TV?
3 He was doing his homework at 11 o'clock.
4 They weren't playing football after school.

c Listen and repeat.
1.19

8 In pairs, ask and answer about yesterday.

What were you doing at 9 o'clock yesterday?

I was taking a shower.

Vocabulary • Adjective + preposition

1 Look at these phrases. Check the meaning in a dictionary. Listen and repeat.
1.20

afraid of	angry with	bad at	bored with
excited about	good at	interested in	popular with
proud of	sorry for	tired of	

Word list page 43
Workbook page 105

2 Match the beginnings (1–5) to the endings (a–e) of the sentences.

1 Karl is excited e
2 I'm afraid
3 He felt sorry
4 She was angry
5 Online videos are very popular

a with her brother because he told a lie.
b for Anna. She looked very sad.
c of snakes and spiders.
d with teenagers.
e about the game tomorrow. He loves basketball!

3 Complete the text with the correct prepositions.

Are you interested ¹ *in* music? Do you like videos? Well, there are a lot of interesting video clips online. Some are funny, and some are silly! People's home videos, especially pets doing funny things, are popular ² .... viewers, too. So if you're good ³ .... making home videos, or you feel proud ⁴ .... a video you made and want to share it, put it online. And when you're bored ⁵ .... video clips and tired ⁶ .... watching people doing silly things, just turn off your computer and do something different!

4 What about you? In pairs, ask and answer.

1 Which school subjects are you interested in?
2 Which sports teams are popular with your friends?
3 What are you afraid of?
4 What achievement are you proud of?

Which school subjects are you interested in?

I'm really interested in history.

Brain Trainer Unit 2 Activity 3
Go to page 113

Unit 2 • What's the Story? 23

Chatroom Permission

Speaking and Listening

1 Look at the photo. Answer the questions.
1 Where are the teenagers?
2 Who are Ruby and Ash looking at?
3 What do you think the attendant is saying?

2 Listen and read the conversation.
1.21 Check your answers.

3 Listen and read again. Answer the questions.
1.21
1 What did Ruby forget?
   She forgot her camera.
2 What does Ash want to do?
3 What can't you do in the museum?
4 What can the teenagers do instead?
5 Why does the attendant stop Ash?
6 Where does Ruby decide to go?

4 Act out the conversation in groups of three.

Ash	Is this your camera, Ruby? You left it on the information desk.
Ruby	Yes, it is. Thanks!
Ash	Do you mind if I use it? My camera is broken. I was taking it out of its case when I dropped it.
Ruby	Of course I don't mind. Go ahead … , but can we take photos in the museum?
Ash	Let's ask. Excuse me, is it OK if we take photos?
Attendant	No, I'm sorry, it isn't.
Ruby	That's too bad. I'm really interested in dinosaurs. But we can buy postcards. Look, there's a gift shop over there.
Ash	Great! I can buy some more chips. This bag is empty.
Attendant	Excuse me. You can't eat in the exhibition hall, but there is a café near the entrance.
Ruby	We can get something to drink there, too. Come on!

Say it in your language …
Go ahead.
That's too bad.

Unit 2 • What's the Story?

5 Look back at the conversation. How do Ash and Ruby ask for permission? How does the attendant refuse permission?

1 Do you …. if …. ? *Do you mind if I use it?*
2 …. OK if …. ?
3 No, I'm …. .

6 Read the phrases for asking for and giving or refusing permission.

Asking for permission	Giving or refusing permission
Can I/we …. ?	Yes, you can./ No, you can't.
Is it OK if I/we/ …. ?	Yes, of course./ No, I'm sorry, it isn't.
Do you mind if I/we … ?	No, I don't mind./ Of course I don't mind./ Yes, I do!

7 Listen to the conversations. Act out
1.22 the conversations in pairs.

Ella	Can I ¹ stay up late tonight, Mom?
Mom	No, you can't. You have school tomorrow.
Tom	Is it OK if I use ² your cell phone? My phone isn't working.
Ash	Sure. Here you go.
Ruby	Do you mind if I ³ read your magazine?
Ella	No, I don't mind.
Tom	Do you mind if I ⁴ send a text message in class?
Teacher	Yes, I do!

8 Work in pairs. Replace the words in purple in Exercise 7. Use these words and/or your own ideas. Act out the conversations.

> Can I watch television, Mom?

> No, you can't. You have school tomorrow.

1 have a party / go out tonight / go to the movies
2 your camera / your laptop / your MP3 player
3 watch TV / play a computer game / play the guitar
4 get to class late / don't do my homework / forget my books

Grammar • Past simple vs Past continuous

(long action)	(short action)
I was taking my camera out of its case	when I dropped it.

(short action)	(long action)
I dropped my camera	while I was taking it out of its case.

Grammar reference Workbook page 88

1 Study the grammar table. Choose the correct options to complete the rules.

1 The Past continuous describes a *long / short* action in progress. The Past simple describes a *long / short* action. This can interrupt the long action.
2 We use *when / while* before a short action and *when / while* before a long action.

2 Complete the sentences. Use the Past simple or Past continuous form of the verbs.

1 We *were taking* (take) pictures when the museum attendant *stopped* (stop) us.
2 He …. (fall down) while he …. (skateboard).
3 She …. (do) her homework when her friend …. (arrive).
4 The doorbell …. (ring) while I …. (take) a bath.
5 We …. (eat) pizza when the movie …. (start).
6 It …. (begin) to rain while they …. (walk) to school.

3 Complete these sentences with your own ideas.

1 I was watching a horror movie when …. .
2 My friends were playing basketball when …. .
3 I was eating a burger when …. .
4 The lights went out while …. .
5 I heard a strange noise while …. .
6 We were sitting on the school bus when …. .

4 Work in pairs. Ask and answer about your sentences in Exercise 3.

> What happened while you were watching a horror movie?

> I saw a face at the window!

Unit 2 • What's the Story? 25

Reading

1 Look at the photos. Answer the questions.

1 What can you see in the photos?
2 Where are the people?
3 What are they doing?

Great Moments in History

This month *World Magazine* is looking at great moments in history. Do you remember these events? What about your parents or grandparents? What's the story behind the picture?

A V-J Day: August 15, 1945

Twenty-seven-year-old Edith Shain was working as a nurse in New York when she heard the news on the radio—the war* was over! All around the US, people were celebrating. Edith was celebrating in Times Square when a sailor kissed her. Edith didn't know the sailor, but she wasn't angry with him. A young photographer was in Times Square, too. He took this photo. A week later Edith saw the photo in *Life* magazine. She was surprised, but she was also proud of the photo!

B Man on the Moon: July 20, 1969

Half a billion people were watching an important event on television. What were they watching? Astronauts Neil Armstrong and Buzz Aldrin. Armstrong was the first man to walk on the moon. "That's one small step for a man, one giant leap for mankind," he said. The two astronauts stayed on the moon for twenty-one hours and collected samples for scientists back on Earth. They left an American flag and some footprints. The flag and footprints are still there today!

C FIFA World Cup Final: June 21, 1970

More than 100,000 people were waiting in Mexico's Azteca soccer stadium. Italy was playing Brazil in the World Cup Final, and Pelé was on the Brazilian team. After the game, a photographer took this picture. It was Pelé's third World Cup win and the first major sports event to appear on TV in color. Millions of people were watching when Pelé lifted the trophy in his yellow soccer shirt!

* World War II (1939–45)

2 Read the magazine article quickly and check your answers to Exercise 1.

3 Read the article again. Copy the table and complete the information. (1.23)

	A	B	C
Event?	V-J Day	….	World Cup Final
When?	….	July 20, 1969	….
Where?	….	….	Mexico
Who?	Edith Shain	….	….

4 Read the article again. Answer the questions. (1.23)

Paragraph A
1 Why did Edith go to Times Square?
2 How did she feel about the sailor?

Paragraph B
3 Why was the event on TV important?
4 What did Armstrong and Aldrin do on the moon?

Paragraph C
5 Why was the 1970 World Cup Final special for Pelé?
6 What was different about this sports event?

Key Words

sailor	kissed	event	leap
mankind	stadium	trophy	

Listening

1 Look at the famous photo on page 118. Answer the questions.

1 What can you see in the photo?
2 When do you think the event happened? 1920s, 1930s, 1950s?

2 Listen to two people talking about the photo and check your answers to Exercise 1. (1.24)

 Listening Bank Unit 2 page 118

Writing • A description of a picture

1 Read the Writing File.

> **Writing File**   Describing a picture
>
> When you describe a picture or a photo, use these phrases to say where things are:
> - in the foreground
> - in the background
> - in the center/middle of the picture
> - on the left/right
> - in the left-hand/right-hand corner

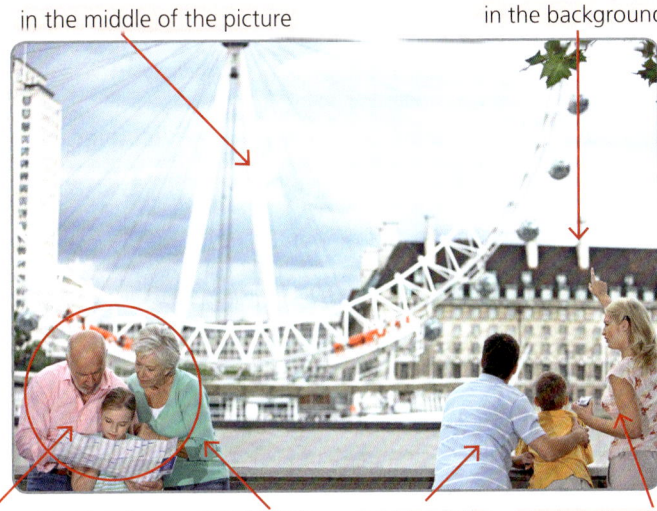

in the middle of the picture   in the background
the foreground   on the left   on the right   in the right-hand corner

2 Read the description. Find four phrases that say where things are.

My Favorite Photo by Jamie

I took this photo on my cell phone last month. It's of a family vacation in Europe with my parents, my sisters, Tara and Marie and my cousin, Joe. We took our dog, Spot, with us, and Joe brought his dog, Rex. The house in the background is Blenheim Palace. It's a little blurry, but it looks dramatic!

Joe and Rex are on the right of the picture. Rex was excited about some birds in a tree. He was barking and Joe was telling him to be quiet. Marie and Tara were laughing because Rex wasn't listening. That's Spot in the foreground of the picture, and Mom and Dad are in the background. Dad was taking a video with his new video camera.

I like this photo because it's funny, and everyone looks happy!

3 Look at Jamie's photo. Are the statements true (T) or false (F)?
1. There's a dog in the left-hand corner.   F
2. There are two people in the center of the picture.
3. There's a palace in the background.
4. There's a man with a video camera on the right.
5. There's a small dog in the foreground.
6. There's a girl on the left.

4 Read the description again. Answer the questions.
1. Where were Jamie and his family?
   They were at Blenheim Palace.
2. When did they go there?
3. Why was Rex barking?
4. What was Jamie's dad doing?
5. Why does Jamie like the photo?

5 Choose an interesting photo of your family or friends. Ask yourself these questions. Take notes.
1. Where is it and why were you there?
2. Who/What is in the photo?
3. Where are the different people in the photo?
4. What were they doing?
5. Why do you like the photo?

6 Write a description of your favorite picture or photo. Use "My favorite photo" and your notes from Exercise 5.

> **My favorite photo**
>
> 1 Introduction: when, where and who
>   *I took this photo …. (when?). I was …. (where?) …. (who with?) …. .*
> 2 Description
>   • what you can see in the photo
>   *…. is on the right of the picture and …. . In the background, there is/are …. .*
>   • what the people were doing
>   *My parents/brother/cousin was/were …. .*
> 3 Conclusion: Why you like the photo

Remember!
- Say where things and people are in your photo.
- Say what people were doing.
- Use the vocabulary in this unit.
- Check your grammar, spelling and punctuation.

Refresh Your Memory!

Grammar • Review

1 Complete the sentences with the Past simple form of these verbs.

> go have make not do not write see send

1 *Did* they *have* English class this morning?
2 I …. you a text message five minutes ago.
3 We …. to the movies last weekend.
4 I …. my homework last night. I was very tired.
5 …. you …. some sandwiches for lunch?
6 She …. her blog last weekend. She didn't have time.
7 He …. a dramatic photo in the newspaper yesterday.

2 Complete the story with the Past continuous form of the verbs.

It was 4:30 p.m. and I [1] *was sitting* (sit) on the school bus with my friend Emma. We [2] …. (not talk) because Emma [3] …. (read) a magazine. I [4] …. (look) out the window. It [5] …. (rain), and people [6] …. (walk) down the street. A girl and a boy [7] …. (stand) near the bus stop, and they [8] …. (laugh). The boy [9] …. (not carry) an umbrella, and his hair was wet. He [10] …. (hold) the girl's hand. I recognized the boy—it was Emma's boyfriend! Then I looked at Emma. She [11] …. (not read) her magazine; she [12] …. (look) out the window, and she [13] …. (not smile).

3 Choose the correct options.

Ben I [1] *called / was calling* you last night. Where were you?
Nina I was at home all evening. What time [2] *did you call / were you calling*?
Ben At 8 o'clock. The phone [3] *rang / was ringing* for a long time!
Nina That's funny. I [4] *didn't hear / wasn't hearing* it.
Ben [5] *Did you sleep / Were you sleeping*?
Nina No, I wasn't. I wasn't tired!
Ben Then what [6] *did you do / were you doing*?
Nina Ah, I remember. I [7] *listened / was listening* to some music on my MP3 player.

Vocabulary • Review

4 Correct the sentences. Use these words.

> dark ~~fake~~ horrible
> interesting old-fashioned silly

1 That's a cheap diamond ring. It's probably **real**. *fake*
2 I love wildlife photos. They're often really **boring**.
3 Matt was **nice** to Sue. He really upset her.
4 It's six o'clock in the evening. It's already **light** outside.
5 It's **sensible** to ride a bike without a helmet.
6 My grandmother's apartment is very **modern**.

5 Complete the sentences with these adjectives.

> afraid angry bad bored
> ~~excited~~ interested popular tired

1 Paolo is very *excited* about his vacation.
2 They were …. with the TV show. It wasn't interesting at all.
3 I'm …. at math. I never get good grades on my homework.
4 Magazines are always …. with girls.
5 Guess what?! Joel is …. of mice!
6 Are you …. in baseball?
7 I'm …. of homework. There's too much to do.
8 I was …. with my brother because he ate my pizza.

Speaking • Review

6 Put the conversation in the correct order (1–6). Then listen and check.
1.25

a Can I have a party on my birthday? 1
b Yes, I do! It's very expensive!
c Do you mind if I take the whole class?
d No, it isn't. You can go to a pizza place.
e Great! Is it OK if I have the party at home, with my friends?
f Hmm … OK. Yes, you can.

Dictation

7 Listen and write in your notebook.
1.26

✓ **My assessment profile:** Workbook page 128

Real World Profiles

Kieron Williamson's Profile

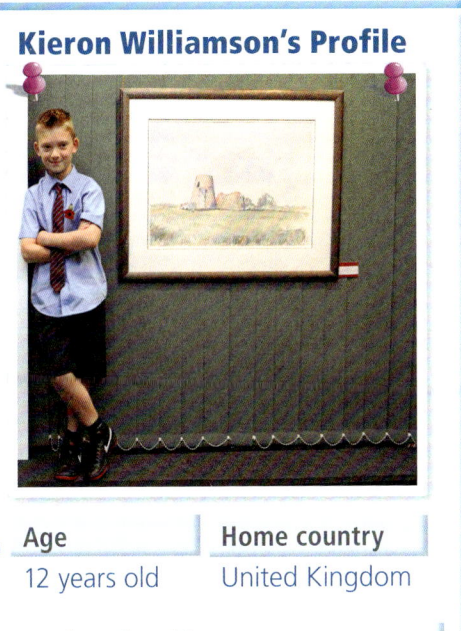

Age: 12 years old
Home country: United Kingdom

My favorite things …
painting, soccer, watching TV, computer games

Kieron's Paintings — Young Artist

He's a famous English artist. He is in the newspapers and on TV, and all the tickets for his last exhibition sold out in fourteen minutes! He's called the new "Picasso" or the "mini-Matisse," and he's only twelve years old. Meet Kieron Williamson.

Kieron was born in 2002 in a town in southeastern England. He lives with his mom, dad and little sister, Billie-Jo. Kieron is a typical boy. He's good at computer games, and he watches TV; he's interested in soccer, and he likes riding his bike. He's also a brilliant artist.

It all started on a family vacation when he was five years old. He was playing on the beach when he saw some boats. He asked his parents for a drawing pad, and the next day he began to draw pictures of the boats. At first his drawings weren't great, but then he started to add background scenery, hills and houses. His pictures got better and better, and he began to ask his parents for advice. Kieron's mom and dad are not artists, so they asked a local artist for help. She gave Kieron lessons, and in August 2009, he had his first exhibition.

Kieron works hard at his art. He gets up at 6 o'clock every morning and paints. His pictures are of the countryside around his town. They're dramatic and colorful, and he paints four or five every week.

People all over the world love Kieron's paintings—and a lot of people are collecting them, so now they cost more than $1,700 each.

Key Words
exhibition   sold out   drawing pad
scenery   countryside

Reading

1 Read Kieron's profile. Complete the sentences.

1 Kieron comes from …. .
2 He's …. old.
3 He likes playing …. and …. .

2 Read the article. Answer the questions.

1.27
1 Which artists is Kieron sometimes compared to?
   He's compared to Picasso and Matisse.
2 Who does he live with?
3 How old was he when he started painting?
4 What was his first painting of?
5 How did his paintings change?
6 Who helped him develop his hobby?
7 What are his paintings like?
8 How much do Kieron's pictures cost?

Class discussion

1 Do you know any famous artists from your country?
2 How old were they when they started painting?
3 Do you know any paintings by Picasso or Matisse? What are they like?

3 It's a Bargain!

Grammar
Comparatives and superlatives; *too* and *enough*; *much, many, a lot of*

Vocabulary
- Shopping nouns;
- Money verbs

Speaking
Asking for help

Writing
A customer review

Word list page 43
Workbook page 106

Vocabulary • Shopping nouns

1 Match the pictures (1–15) to these words. Then listen, check and repeat.
1.28

ATM
bargain
bill
change
coin
customer
line
mall
market stand
price *1*
products
sale
salesperson
shopping basket
vendor

2 Complete the conversation with the words in Exercise 1.

Dean This is my favorite store in the ¹ *mall*.
Louis I love this coat, but how much is it?
Dean Ask the ² .... . She'll know.
Louis Oh! It's $17. It's on ³ .... for half price.
Dean It's a ⁴ .... ! Are you going to buy it?
Louis Yes, but I need to go to the ⁵ .... first. I only have a ⁶ .... or two, and I can't buy a coat with that!
Dean But there's always a long ⁷ .... at the ATM. Here's a twenty-dollar ⁸ .... . You can get some money later.

3 Complete the sentences with the words in Exercise 1.

1 The *price* of gas is very high.
2 This grocery store sells really good ....—they often buy from the local farmers.
3 Salespeople should always make sure they give the .... the correct .... when they buy something.

4 In pairs, ask and answer about your local area.

1 Where or when are there good bargains?
2 Which stores have friendly salespeople?
3 Where or when are there often lines?

Brain Trainer Unit 3
Activity 2
Go to page 113

Unit 3 • It's a Bargain!

Reading

1 Look at the photos. Do you think these statements are true (T) or false (F)?
1. The market is very old. *T*
2. Now it's only popular with older people.
3. It sells fresh food.
4. The prices are high.

2 Read the magazine article and check your answers to Exercise 1.
1.29

3 Read the article again. Match the headings (A–D) to the paragraphs (1–4).
A The market has a long history.
B Today that is difficult to believe.
C Shopping is often more interesting at the market, too.
D Haymarket vendors have plenty of loyal customers. *1*

4 Answer the questions.
1. What are Haymarket vendors happy about?
   Their market is becoming more popular.
2. What do locals like about Haymarket?
3. Why did people think the market might disappear?
4. What does Nick like about the products at the market?
5. What advice does Stacy give about the food from the market?

5 What about you? Answer the questions.
1. What are the markets like in your area?
2. How often do you go to a market?
3. What do you buy there?
4. What do you like/dislike about markets?

News | Boston

Boston Market Wins More Customers

Haymarket vendors have a reason to celebrate. Their market is becoming more popular than ever.

1 .... "This is the busiest market in Boston!" says Vicky Green at her fruit stand. "All the locals come here because it's very close to downtown. It also has convenient hours and the best prices in Boston!"

2 .... For hundreds of years, Haymarket has been the best place to buy fruits and vegetables in Boston. Vendors started gathering in this area of Boston's North End in the mid-1700s. The market grew larger in the nineteenth and twentieth centuries, but almost disappeared when highway construction disrupted the street in the 1990s.

3 .... The street is now filled with produce stands selling fruits and vegetables from all over the world. And customers love it. "Prices here are often cheaper than in the grocery store, so you can find some great bargains," explains Nick Baines, 16. This is because vendors sell the produce that nearby

wholesalers weren't able to sell to grocery stores. "Just remember that the fruits and vegetables are usually very ripe," says Stacy Mills, 30, "so you need to eat them soon. But you can get a lot of produce for a great price. And the vendors are much friendlier than salespeople in a supermarket."

4 .... "In every grocery store you always find the same products," says Eileen Fisher, 21. "I prefer Haymarket because I can get some really exotic food here, for example, from Asia or North Africa. And there are many market stands to choose from."

The future has never looked better for Haymarket. It has truly become a Boston tradition!

Unit 3 • It's a Bargain! 31

Grammar • Comparatives and superlatives

Adjective	Comparative	Superlative
cheap	cheaper	cheapest
nice	nicer	nicest
big	bigger	biggest
friendly	friendlier	friendliest
interesting	more interesting	most interesting
good	better	best
bad	worse	worst
far	farther	farthest

Market vendors are *friendlier than* salespeople.
Haymarket is *the busiest* market in Boston!

Grammar reference Workbook page 90

1 Study the grammar table and the examples. Complete the rules with *comparative* or *superlative*.

1 We compare two people or things with the …. .
2 We compare one person or thing to the rest of its group with the …. .
3 We use *the* before the …. .
4 We use *than* after the …. .

2 Complete the sentences with the correct form of the adjectives.

1 We're *hungrier* (hungry) than you.
2 August is the …. (hot) month of the year.
3 It is the …. (large) market in Boston.
4 The T-shirt is …. (clean) than the jacket.
5 My sister's …. (selfish) than my brother.
6 This is the …. (bad) day of my life!

3 Complete the text with the correct form of the adjectives.

The ¹ *most popular* (popular) markets in Thailand are on water, and the stands are boats. Taling Chan is the ² …. (good) market near the city of Bangkok, but the ³ …. (big) and ⁴ …. (busy) market in Thailand is at Ratchaburi. It is ⁵ …. (far) from Bangkok than Taling Chan, and prices there are ⁶ …. (expensive) than prices in other places. Why? Because this market is one of the ⁷ …. (famous) and ⁸ …. (exciting) markets in the world!

• *Too* and *enough*

The jeans are *too expensive*.
The jeans are*n't cheap enough*.
I don't have *enough money* for the jeans.

Grammar reference Workbook page 90

4 Study the grammar table. Complete the rules with *too* or *enough*.

1 We use …. + adjective.
2 We use *(not)* adjective + …. .
3 We use …. + noun.

5 Make sentences and questions.

1 aren't / people / There / enough
   There aren't enough people.
2 you / too / tired / Are / ?
3 fast / enough / It / isn't
4 She / too / works / always / hard

6 Complete the second sentence so it means the same as the first. Use the word in parentheses.

1 That color is too bright. (dark)
   That color *isn't dark enough*.
2 The shopping basket is too heavy. (light)
   The shopping basket …. .
3 The movie wasn't exciting enough for me. (boring)
   The movie …. for me.
4 Our baseball team is too small. (players)
   We don't have …. on our baseball team.
5 The library is never quiet enough. (noisy)
   The library is always …. .

7 **What about you?** Make sentences about different stores, shopping areas or markets where you live. Use comparatives, superlatives, *too* and *enough*. Use some of these adjectives.

big	busy	cheap	cool
expensive	good	interesting	noisy
old	quiet	small	

> The mall is busiest on Saturdays.

> There aren't enough clothing stores downtown.

Unit 3 • It's a Bargain!

Vocabulary • Money verbs

1 Match the pictures (1–12) to these verb pairs. Then listen, check and repeat.
1.30

buy/sell 1–2	cost/afford
lend/borrow	pay in cash/pay by credit card
save/spend	win/earn

Word list page 43
Workbook page 106

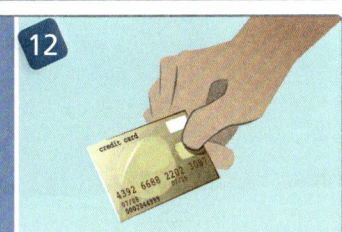

2 Complete the sentences with the correct verbs.

borrow/lend	~~cost/afford~~	in cash/by credit card
saved/spent	sells/buys	won/earns

1 The DVDs *cost* $20. I can't *afford* one. I don't have enough money.
2 The vendor …. fruit and vegetables. The customer …. her fruit from him.
3 Sam took out a bill from his wallet and paid for the sandwiches …. . Ellie didn't have any cash, so she paid for her lunch …. .
4 They sometimes …. their dad's laptop. But he doesn't always …. it to them.
5 Tara …. her money in the bank, so she has $500 now. Todd …. all his money on computer games, so he doesn't have any money now.
6 Daniel …. $100 in a contest last week. Olivia only …. $100 a week.

Pronunciation /ɔ/ and /oʊ/

3a Listen and repeat.
1.31

/ɔ/	/oʊ/
cost	go
long	home
on	show

b Listen and repeat. Then practice saying the sentences.
1.32

1 Go home on the boat.
2 Can I borrow your orange coat?
3 The vendor sold me some old posters.

4 Match the beginnings (1–5) to the endings (a–e) of the sentences.

1 My favorite store sells   a save for it.
2 I usually spend my money   b by credit card.
3 I sometimes borrow money   c pet snakes.
4 I usually pay for new clothes   d from my dad.
5 If I can't afford something nice, I   e on DVDs.

5 Look at the sentence beginnings (1–5) in Exercise 4. Complete the sentences so they are true for you.

**Brain Trainer Unit 3
Activity 3**
Go to page 113

Unit 3 • It's a Bargain!

Chatroom Asking for help

Speaking and Listening

1 Look at the photo. What does Ella want to buy?

2 Listen and read the conversation.
1.33 Check your answer.

3 Listen and read again. Answer the questions.
1.33
1. What help does Tom give Ella?
   He helps her with her bags.
2. Why does Ella want the T-shirt?
3. When does Ella want to buy the T-shirt?
4. Can the salesperson save the T-shirt for Ella?
5. Why does Ella ask Tom about his money?
6. Does Tom think the T-shirt is a bargain?

4 Act out the conversation in groups of three.

Ella	Hey, Tom. Can you give me a hand with these bags?
Tom	Sure.
Ella	Thanks. I want to look at these T-shirts.
Tom	But you have a lot of T-shirts, Ella. You don't need a new one.
Ella	I don't have many nice T-shirts. These are nicer than all my clothes at home. Oh look, there's the salesperson … Excuse me, would you mind saving this for me until next week?
Salesperson	Sorry, I can't. It's against the rules.
Ella	That's too bad. Er, Tom … how much money do you have?
Tom	Why?
Ella	Well, I can't afford any new clothes right now. Could you lend me some money?
Tom	No problem. How much?
Ella	$30.
Tom	$30 is too much money for one T-shirt!
Ella	But for $30 I can buy five T-shirts.
Tom	Oh, Ella! You're impossible!

Say it in your language …
It's against the rules.
You're impossible!

5 Look back at the conversation. Complete the sentences.

1 Can you *give me a hand* with these bags?
2 .... saving this for me until next week?
3 .... lend me some money?

6 Read the phrases for asking for help. Find three responses in the conversation.

Asking for help	Responding
Could you … ?	OK.
Can you …?	Sure.
Can/Could you give me a hand with …?	No problem.
Would you mind …-ing …?	Sorry, I can't.

7 Listen to the conversations. Does each person agree to help or not? Act out the conversations in pairs.
1.34

Ruby Can you lend me ¹ a pen?
Ella Sorry, I can't. I only have one.
Ash Could you give me a hand with ² this homework?
Ruby Sorry, I can't.
Ella Would you mind ³ carrying my bag?
Tom No problem.

8 Work in pairs. Replace the words in purple in Exercise 7. Use these words and/or your own ideas. Act out the conversations.

> Can you lend me a calculator?

> Sorry, I can't. I only have one.

1 a pencil / a ruler / an eraser
2 my English / these sandwiches / this computer
3 taking a photo / opening the door / coming with me

Grammar • Much, many, a lot of

How much money does she have?	How many T-shirts does she have?
She has a lot of money.	She has a lot of T-shirts.
She doesn't have much/a lot of money.	She doesn't have many/a lot of T-shirts.
She has too much money.	She has too many T-shirts.

Grammar reference Workbook page 90

1 Study the grammar table. Complete the rules with *(too) much*, *(too) many* or *a lot of*.

1 With countable nouns, we use *a lot of* or .... .
2 With uncountable nouns, we use *a lot of* or .... .
3 In affirmative sentences, we usually use .... .
4 In negative sentences, we can use ...., ... or .... .

2 Choose the correct options.

1 There are too *much / many* people here.
2 He doesn't make *much / many* money.
3 She does *a lot of / much* homework every night.
4 How *much / many* credit cards do you have?
5 I ate too *much / many* food yesterday.
6 He took *a lot of / too much* photos.

3 Complete the text with *much*, *many* or *a lot of*.

How ¹ *many* underground stores are there in your city or town? In Toronto, Canada, there are 1,200! In the winter there's ² .... snow in Toronto, and people don't spend ³ .... time outside in the cold. In the summer, there are too ⁴ .... cars on the streets and too ⁵ .... pollution. So, instead, ⁶ .... people like shopping on the 28 km of paths under the city.

4 In pairs, ask and answer about these things.

| cash in your wallet | free time | homework |
| shoes | T-shirts | |

> How much free time do you have?

> I have a lot of free time.

Unit 3 • It's a Bargain! 35

Reading

1 Look at the heading and the photos. What connection do you think the photos have to the text?

The Internet

The Internet—the World's Biggest Market

1 …. A lot of people find shopping online easier than going to their local mall or to the supermarket, and they love the cheaper prices on the Internet. They also like reading other customers' reviews so they know different people's opinions about a product before they buy it. But for many people, the most important advantage of online shopping is the choice.

2 …. Shopping in your city or town isn't easy if you don't like the same things as everyone else. That isn't a problem online. On the Internet, your shopping mall is the world. You can buy from a Korean music store, a Mexican chili farmer and a Nigerian hat designer all in one afternoon.

3 …. The Internet is also the perfect place to find something strange or unusual. You can buy a jar of Alaskan snow, the poster for a 1920s horror movie or a potato in the shape of a rabbit! Soon after singer Justin Bieber went to the hairstylist, a fan bought a small box of his hair at an auction website for $40,668!

4 …. For some people, experiences are more important than possessions, and they too can find a lot of interesting things on the Internet. Would you like to give your name to a character in a novel or appear in a TV show? Win the right online auction and you can. In 2008, someone even bought an evening with actor Scarlett Johansson for $40,100 (the money went to the charity Oxfam).

You don't get much exercise when you shop online, and you don't see many friendly faces, but if you are looking for something unusual, there's nowhere better!

Key Words

| advantage | fan | auction |
| character | novel | charity |

2 Read the text quickly and check your ideas.

3 Read the text again. Match the headings (A–D)
1.35 to the paragraphs (1–4).

A An experience to remember
B International shopping
C Why shop online? *1*
D No one else has that!

4 Read the text again. Answer the questions.

1 How do online shoppers know if other customers like a product? *They read their reviews.*
2 Why is it difficult for some people to find nice things in their city or town?
3 Why did someone pay $40,668 for a box of hair?
4 How, according to the text, can the Internet help you to be on TV?
5 What are the disadvantages of online shopping?

5 In pairs, compare shopping on the Internet with shopping in your local mall.

> How much do you buy on the Internet?

> I buy about two things online every month.

Listening

1 What problems do people sometimes have when they buy things online? Make a list.

2 Listen to the news report. Was the boy's problem
1.36 one of the things on your list in Exercise 1?

 Listening Bank Unit 3 page 118

Unit 3 • It's a Bargain!

Writing • A customer review

1 Read the Writing File.

> **Writing File** Expressing opinion
>
> **You can introduce your opinion with:**
>
> I think (that) those boots are a waste of money.
> I don't think (that) it's a very useful bag.
> In my opinion, it's too expensive.
> I find it very difficult to use.

2 Read a customer's online review of a camera. Find three phrases that express an opinion.

Search: digital camera

iPix S70 Blue $150
Other colors available

Your reviews

The iPix S70 camera costs $150 on sale. It comes in a choice of six different colors.
The camera is only 10 cm long and it's very light, so it fits in a small bag easily. It takes great photos inside and outside, and it can make short videos, too. I find it very easy to use.
However, it has some problems. When you take a photo of something too near to the camera, the quality of the photo isn't very good. Another problem is the size of the screen. It isn't big enough if you want to look at your photos on the camera.
In my opinion, the iPix S70 isn't the best small camera available. However, for $150, I think it's a good bargain.

3 Complete the sentences with these phrases.

| I don't think | I find it | I think | In my opinion |

1 I love this book. *I find it* very interesting.
2 I really don't want that poster. …. that it's very nice.
3 I never go there. …. it's the worst store in town.
4 …. , outdoor markets sell the freshest food.

4 Read the review again and answer the questions.

1 How much does the camera cost?
   It costs $150 on sale.
2 Is there a choice (e.g., of size, color, etc.)?
3 Is its size a good thing or a bad thing? Why?
4 What can you do with it?
5 Is it easy to use?
6 What problems does it have?
7 What is the writer's general opinion of it?

5 You are going to write a customer review of one of these products: a cell phone, an MP3 player or a bag. Use the questions in Exercise 4 to help you. Take notes.

6 Write your customer review. Use "My review" and your notes from Exercise 5.

> **My review**
>
> **Paragraph 1**
> Introduce the product. Say how much it costs and what choices there are (color, size, etc.).
>
> **Paragraph 2**
> Describe the product. Say what you like about it.
>
> **Paragraph 3**
> Describe any problems with the product.
>
> **Paragraph 4**
> Summarize your opinion of the product.

> **Remember!**
> - Express opinions with expressions from the Writing File.
> - Use the vocabulary and grammar you've practiced in this unit.
> - Check your grammar, spelling and punctuation.

Unit 3 • It's a Bargain!

Refresh Your Memory!

Grammar • Review

1 Make eight sentences comparing the stores in the table. Use the comparative or superlative form of these adjectives.

> bad big cheap expensive
> friendly good large popular

	Dollar Stop	Fashionista	Mason's
Size	2,000 m²	900 m²	3,500 m²
Prices	Everything $1	$2–$99	$50–$29,999
Customers per week	5,000	12,000	2,000
Salespeople	unfriendly	very friendly	friendly
Products	not very good	OK	very good

Fashionista is the most popular shop.
Mason's has friendlier salespeople than Dollar Stop.

2 Make sentences.

1 doesn't / She / enough / friends / have
  She doesn't have enough friends.
2 enough / T-shirt / The / big / isn't
3 The / too / expensive / are / scarves
4 is / market / too / The / noisy
5 money / don't / enough / We / earn
6 aren't / enough / My / fashionable / clothes

3 Complete the conversation with *a lot of, much* or *many*.

A I don't have ¹ *many* summer clothes, so I'm going shopping.
B Oh, I need ² …. things downtown. Can I give you a list? I can't go with you because I have too ³ …. homework.
A OK, if you're quick. I don't have ⁴ …. time. There's a bus in five minutes, and you know there aren't ⁵ …. buses on the weekend.
B Thanks. Here's the list. I hope there aren't too ⁶ …. things.
A What? How ⁷ …. hands do you think I have?! I can't carry all this!

Vocabulary • Review

4 Match these words to the definitions (1–5).

> ~~ATM~~ bargain coin
> customer sale

1 You use a card to get money from this. *ATM*
2 This type of money is small and hard.
3 When a store has this, the prices are cheaper.
4 This person buys things in stores.
5 This is a product with a cheap price.

5 One of the underlined words in each sentence is incorrect. Correct it.

1 "How much do the jeans ~~spend~~?" *cost*
  "Ten dollars. They're a very good price."
2 He wins a lot of money at his market stand because he sells really popular things.
3 Do you want to pay in cash or with credit card?
4 He can't cost designer clothes at the mall in his town.
5 Can I lend a ten-dollar bill so I can buy my train ticket?

Speaking • Review

6 Complete the conversations with these words. Then listen and check. *1.37*

> can ~~could~~ give mind
> problem sorry sure with

A ¹ *Could* you lend me your cell phone for a minute, please?
B ² …. . Here you go.

A Would you ³ …. carrying the shopping basket?
B OK. No ⁴ …. .

A ⁵ …. you ⁶ …. me a hand ⁷ …. the food?
B ⁸ …. , I can't. I'm too busy.

Dictation

7 Listen and write in your notebook. *1.38*

✓ **My assessment profile:** Workbook page 129

Unit 3 • It's a Bargain!

Math File

Prices of Products Around the World

Do you pay more for products than people in other countries? Look at this table and find out.

	The UK	China	The US	France
(ticket)	£8.00 (€…)	¥30.00 (€…)	$9.00 (€…)	€6.20
(burger)	£2.20 (€…)	¥14.50 (€…)	$3.60 (€…)	€3.50
(magazine)	£3.50 (€…)	¥5.00 (€…)	$3.50 (€…)	€2.40
(sneakers)	£60.00 (€…)	¥388.00 (€…)	$55.00 (€…)	€50.00

Do the math

Do you know how to change one currency into another? Use our easy guide.
First, you must know the exchange rate. Exchange rates change every day. You can find them online or in a newspaper, or in banks and post offices.
Then do the math.

Price in currency A **x**
Exchange rate for 1 unit of currency A **=**
Price in currency B

For example:
Price of a burger in South Africa = 17 rand
Exchange rate: 1 rand = 0.10 euros
How much does the burger cost in euros?
17 x 0.10 = 1.70
The burger costs 1.70 euros.

Key Words
currency   exchange rate

Reading

1 Match the currencies to the countries. What is your country's currency?

pound (£)   dollar ($)
yuan (¥)   euro (€)
rand (R)

China   France
South Africa   The UK
The US

2 Read the magazine article and answer the questions.
1 How much do sneakers cost in the US?
 $55.00
2 In which country is a magazine more expensive than a burger?
3 How many magazines can you buy for the price of a movie ticket in China?
4 Name two places where you can find out about exchange rates.

3 Calculate the price in euros of the items from the UK, China and the US in the table in the article. Use the exchange rates below.

exchange rates	
£1	€1.20
¥1	€0.10
US$1	€0.75

4 Listen. Are these statements true (T) or false (F)?
1.39 Use your euro prices from Exercise 3 to help you.

My Math File

5 Find out the price of three items in your country and in two other countries with a different currency. Convert the prices into your currency.

6 Make a poster with the information from Exercise 5. Include a table like the one in the article and sentences comparing the items.

Switzerland has the most expensive coffee.
Tickets to soccer games are cheaper in Mexico than in my country.

Unit 3 • It's a Bargain!

Review 1

Grammar • Present simple and continuous

1 Complete the conversation with the Present simple or Present continuous form of the verbs.

A ¹ *Do* you *want* (want) to go out with us tonight? We ² .... (go) to Pat's house after her music lesson. You know she ³ .... (have) a music lesson at 5 p.m. on Fridays. Then we ⁴ .... (go) out for pizza at 6 p.m.

B Oh, I ⁵ .... (play) a tennis match at that time. We always ⁶ .... (have) matches on Friday nights. But I'm free tomorrow. What ⁷ .... you .... ? (do)

A Well, I usually ⁸ .... (go) swimming, but tomorrow I ⁹ .... (meet) Jane at the café. Why don't you join us?

B Good idea. I ¹⁰ .... (go) to the mall anyway, so I can meet you afterward.

• Verb + -ing

2 Make sentences.

1 Do / you like / get up / early?
   Do you like getting up early?
2 I / prefer / watch movies to plays.
3 Jenny / hate / do housework.
4 My mom / really enjoy / work in the yard.
5 I / not mind / clean up / my room. But I / hate / iron.

• Past simple

3 Complete the conversation with the Past simple form of the verbs.

A What ¹ *did* you *do* (do) on the weekend?
B I ² .... (go) shopping.
A What ³ .... you .... ? (buy)
B I ⁴ .... (buy) a birthday present for my friend. She ⁵ .... (have) a party on Saturday night.
A ⁶ .... (be) it a good party?
B Yes! Her brother's band ⁷ .... (play), and we all ⁸ .... (dance). I ⁹ .... (give) her a CD, and we ¹⁰ .... (listen) to that, too.
A What time ¹¹ .... the party .... ? (end)
B I ¹² .... (come) home at about 11 p.m. But I think the party ¹³ .... (end) at midnight!

• Past continuous

4 Complete the text with the Past continuous forms of the verbs.

Yesterday, everyone in our house ¹ *was doing* (do) something different. My brother and his friends ² .... (play) soccer in the backyard. My dad ³ .... (fix) his bike. My mom ⁴ .... (make) a cake and ⁵ .... (listen) to the radio. And me? I ⁶ .... (lie) on my bed and ⁷ .... (read) my favorite magazine! What ⁸ .... you .... ? (do)

• Past simple vs past continuous

5 Choose the correct option.

1 I *was texting* / *texted* my friend while I *was walking* / *walked* down the street. Then I *was walking* / *walked* into a tree!
2 We *were watching* / *watched* a movie on TV when suddenly it *stopped* / *was stopping* working. So we *weren't seeing* / *didn't see* the end of the movie.
3 It *was raining* / *rained* yesterday, so we *weren't having* / *didn't have* a picnic.
4 While I *was waiting* / *waited* at the dentist's, I *was reading* / *read* magazines.
5 I *was sitting* / *sat* in a café when I suddenly *was seeing* / *saw* an old friend.
6 I *was hurting* / *hurt* my ankle yesterday. I *was standing* / *stood* on a chair to reach the top shelf when I *was falling* / *fell*.

• Comparatives and superlatives

6 Make sentences using the correct form of the adjectives.

1 A whale / heavy / an elephant.
   A whale is heavier than an elephant.
2 The cheetah is / fast / animal in the world.
3 Which is / big—London or Paris?
4 I think Adam Sandler is / funny / actor in Hollywood.
5 That was / good / pizza / in the world!
6 My math test was / bad / my English test.
7 Tracy lives / far / from school / me.
8 The weather today is / good / yesterday.

- **Too and enough**

7 Complete the second sentence so that it means the same as the first. Use the word in parentheses.

1 You aren't old enough to drive. (young)
  You are too young to drive.
2 I'm too short to reach that shelf. (tall)
3 You are too sick to go to school today. (well)
4 He isn't strong enough to lift that heavy box. (weak)
5 This T-shirt is too small for me. (big)
6 The tickets are too expensive. (cheap)
7 That theme park ride was boring. It was too slow! (fast)
8 We arrived too late to get the best seats in the theater. (early)

- **Much, many, a lot of**

8 Complete the sentences with *much, many* or *a lot of*.

1 How *much* do you know about Philadelphia?
2 Do you know, for example, how …. neighborhoods there are?
3 They're planning to build a new library at our school. There's …. work to do.
4 Let's go somewhere else to eat. There are too …. people at this restaurant.
5 I can't buy that jacket. It costs too …. .
6 Wow! You have so …. DVDs!
7 We don't need any more juice. There's …. juice left in the bottle.
8 How …. time do we have before class starts?

Speaking • Describing a place

1 Put the conversation in the correct order.

..1.. What's your new house like?
…. Yes. There are a lot of flowers and trees in it.
…. Is it big?
…. Is the backyard nice?
…. It's great!
…. Yes. It's bigger than our old house.
When can I come and see it?
Come today, after school!

- **Permission**

2 Complete the conversation with these words.

| sorry | ~~can~~ | can't | do | mind | OK |

Paul   ¹ *Can* I go out with Alex tonight, Mom?
Mom No, you ² …. . You have to do your homework.
Paul   Well, is it ³ …. if I go out after that?
Mom Yes, you can. But don't stay out too late.
Paul   Er … Alex lives really far away. Do you ⁴ …. if I stay over at Alex's house tonight?
Mom Yes, I ⁵ …. ! You can't stay over on a school night.
Paul   Well, can you give me a ride home?
Mom No, I'm ⁶ …. Paul. Maybe you should stay at home after all.

- **Asking for help**

3 Choose the correct option.

A Could you give me a ¹ *hand* / *lend* with this heavy box, Steve?
B ² *Sorry.* / *Sure.*
A Thanks. ³ *Would* / *Can* you mind ⁴ *carry* / *carrying* it to the station for me?
B Sorry, I ⁵ *don't* / *can't*. I'm meeting my friend in five minutes and we're going to watch a basketball game.
A Well, could you just carry it to the end of the block?
B ⁶ *No problem.* / *Not sure.* You can take a taxi from there.

Vocabulary • Rooms and parts of the house

1 Complete the words for rooms and parts of the house.

1 There is an a *t t i* c at the top of the house.
2 Walk down the s _ _ _ rs to the b _ s _ m _ _ t, below the house.
3 We don't have a yard, but we have a small p _ _ _ o.
4 We park the car in the g _ r _ _ e.
5 Our front d _ _ r is red.
6 The rooms have very high c _ _ l _ _ gs.
7 My father works from home. He uses one room as his o _ f _ ce.

Review 1   41

Review 1

- ## Furniture and household objects

    2 Match the words on the left (1–10) to the words on the right (a–j) to make furniture and household objects.

    1 alarm   a case
    2 dress   b chair
    3 clos   c clock
    4 arm   d er
    5 cur   e ions
    6 book   f low
    7 cush   g et
    8 pil   h ror
    9 comf   i tains
    10 mir   j orter

- ## Adjectives to describe pictures

    3 Complete the sentences with these adjectives.

    | awful | beautiful | blurry | boring |
    | colorful | fake | funny | ~~interesting~~ |
    | old-fashioned | silly | | |

    1 It doesn't look very *interesting*—it looks pretty boring.
    2 The photo isn't very clear. It's .... .
    3 The colors are kind of .... . They're just gray and brown.
    4 I love this picture—especially the .... red, orange and yellow flowers.
    5 This picture makes me laugh. It's very .... .
    6 It isn't a modern picture. It's very .... .
    7 Is it a real photo, or is it .... ?
    8 It isn't serious. It's .... .
    9 The picture of the park is ....—it's very pretty.
    10 What an ugly place! It looks really .... .

- ## Adjective + preposition

    4 Complete the sentences with the correct preposition.

    a If you get bored ¹ *with* the music on your MP3 player, try downloading radio podcasts instead. There are podcasts for all kinds of shows. If you are interested ² .... plays, you can listen to stories or dramas, too. I get tired ³ .... the same old music, so I sometimes listen to an online radio station.
    b We're going to a theme park this weekend! I'm really excited ⁴ .... that. I'm not afraid ⁵ .... fast and dangerous rides. I love them!
    c I hope I do well on my exams. I want my parents to be proud ⁶ .... me. I don't want them to be angry ⁷ .... me.

- ## Shopping nouns

    5 Complete the sentences with these words.

    | ATM | bargains | bill | coins |
    | customers | sale | salesperson | stand |

    1 You can take money out of an *ATM*.
    2 When a store has a .... , things are cheaper, and you can find a lot of .... .
    3 A .... works in a store and helps the .... .
    4 I have a ten dollar .... and some fifty cents in .... in my pocket.
    5 He sells fruits and vegetables at the market. His .... is near the entrance.

- ## Money verbs

    6 Choose the correct option.

    The City Market is a very popular market in Kansas City, Missouri. People come there from all over the state to ¹ *buy* / *borrow* things. Most items aren't expensive, so you can find something you can ² *cost* / *afford*. Markets are cheaper than stores in the mall, so you can ³ *save* / *win* some money. But vendors want you to pay ⁴ *in* / *by* cash. They don't have machines for ⁵ *credit* / *spend* cards. If you want to go to the market, I'll ⁶ *borrow* / *lend* you a big shopping bag. You'll need it for all your bargains!

Word list

Unit 1 • Home Sweet Home

Rooms and parts of the house

attic	/ˈæt̬ɪk/
balcony	/ˈbælkəni/
basement	/ˈbeɪsmənt/
ceiling	/ˈsilɪŋ/
driveway	/ˈdraɪvweɪ/
fireplace	/ˈfaɪɚpleɪs/
floor	/flɔr/
garage	/gəˈrɑʒ/
hallway	/ˈhɔlweɪ/
landing	/ˈlændɪŋ/
office	/ˈɔfɪs/
patio	/ˈpæt̬i‚oʊ/
roof	/ruf/
stairs	/stɛrz/
wall	/wɔl/
yard	/yɑrd/

Furniture and household objects

alarm clock	/əˈlɑrm ˌklɑk/
armchair	/ˈɑrmtʃɛr/
blind	/blaɪnd/
bookcase	/ˈbʊk-keɪs/
closet	/ˈklɑzɪt/
comforter	/ˈkʌmfət̬ɚ/
curtain	/ˈkɚtˀn/
cushion	/ˈkʊʃən/
dresser	/ˈdrɛsɚ/
mirror	/ˈmɪrɚ/
pillow	/ˈpɪloʊ/
rug	/rʌg/
vase	/veɪs/

Unit 2 • What's the Story?

Adjectives to describe pictures

beautiful	/ˈbyut̬əfəl/
blurry	/ˈblɚi/
boring	/ˈbɔrɪŋ/
colorful	/ˈkʌləfəl/
dark	/dɑrk/
dramatic	/drəˈmæt̬ɪk/
fake	/feɪk/
funny	/ˈfʌni/
horrible	/ˈhɔrəbəl/
interesting	/ˈɪntrɪstɪŋ/
old-fashioned	/ˌoʊld ˈfæʃənd/
silly	/ˈsɪli/

Adjective + preposition

afraid of	/əˈfreɪd əv/
angry with	/ˈæŋgri wɪð, wɪθ/
bad at	/ˈbæd ət/
bored with	/bɔrd wɪð, wɪθ/
excited about	/ɪkˈsaɪt̬ɪd əˌbaʊt/
good at	/ˈgʊd ət/
interested in	/ˈɪntrɪstɪd ɪn/
popular with	/ˈpɑpyəlɚ wɪð, wɪθ/
proud of	/ˈpraʊd əv/
sorry for	/ˈsɑri fɚ, fɔr/
tired of	/ˈtaɪɚd əv/

Unit 3 • It's a Bargain!

Shopping nouns

ATM	/ˌeɪ ti ˈɛm/
bargain	/ˈbɑrgən/
bill	/bɪl/
change	/tʃeɪndʒ/
coin	/kɔɪn/
customer	/ˈkʌstəmɚ/
line	/laɪn/
mall	/mɔl/
market stand	/ˈmɑrkɪt ˌstænd/
price	/praɪs/
products	/ˈprɑdʌkts/
sale	/seɪl/
salesperson	/ˈseɪlzˌpɚsən/
shopping basket	/ˈʃɑpɪŋ ˌbæskɪt/
vendor	/ˈvɛndɚ/

Money verbs

afford	/əˈfɔrd/
borrow	/ˈbɑroʊ/
buy	/baɪ/
cost	/kɔst/
earn	/ɚn/
lend	/lɛnd/
pay by credit card	/peɪ baɪ ˈkrɛdɪt kɑrd/
pay in cash	/peɪ ɪn ˈkæʃ/
save	/seɪv/
sell	/sɛl/
spend	/spɛnd/
win	/wɪn/

4 In the News

Grammar
Present perfect; Present perfect vs Past simple

Vocabulary
News and media; Adverbs of manner

■ **Speaking**
■ Doubt and disbelief

Writing
A profile

Word list page 77
Workbook page 107

Vocabulary • News and media

1 Match the pictures (1–4) to three or four of these words and complete the table. Then listen, check and repeat.

blog
current affairs show
headline
international news
interview (n, v)
journalist
local news
national news
news anchor
news flash
newspaper
news website
podcast
report (n, v)

2 Complete the sentences with the words in Exercise 1.

1 The *headlines* in today's *newspapers* are all about the football game.
2 I'd love to be a …. on TV or for a newspaper and …. important people.
3 I want to start a …. on the Internet so I can write about my vacations.
4 I often read *Teen News* on my computer. It's a …. for teenagers.
5 I don't usually download …. , but this one is interesting. It's an interview with Justin Bieber.
6 My uncle's a …. . He reads the news on a …. .

3 In pairs, ask and answer.

1 Do you prefer to read the news in a newspaper or online?
2 What was the last news story you read about?
3 Can you name any news anchors?
4 Do you prefer local news or international news?

1	2	3	4
news anchor	…..		
…..	…..	…..	
…..	…..	…..	
…..			

I prefer reading a newspaper. What about you?

I like reading news online—it's quicker!

Brain Trainer Unit 4
Activity 2
Go to page 114

Unit 4 • In the News

Reading

1 You are going to read a survey about teens and the news. Look at the photo and answer the questions.

1 What is the girl doing?
2 What do you think she is reading about?
3 Do your family or friends read a print newspaper?

2 Can you predict the results of the survey? Complete the sentences with these numbers.

~~85~~   51   35   31   16   69

_85_ % of teenagers watch news flashes about important events
.... % of teenagers watch the news on TV.
.... % log on to news websites.
.... % read the news every day.
.... % watch current affairs shows.
.... % could live without newspapers.

3 Read the survey quickly and check your answers to Exercise 2.

4 Read the survey again. Answer the questions.

1 What type of news are teens interested in?
   National news.
2 How many teens think newspapers are important?
3 How did Jake find out about the tsunami in Japan?
4 Why does he like news websites?
5 Why hasn't Lisa read the news this week?
6 Where does she usually read a newspaper?
7 Which stories does she read?

5 **What about you?** In pairs, ask and answer the four questions in the survey.

Survey: Teens and the Media

In last month's issue of *Teen News,* we asked you to mail us your answers to the following questions:

- Have you read or heard today's news headlines?
- Where do you usually get your news from?
- Do you read or listen to the news every day?
- What news are you interested in?

Here are the results!

Most of you (sixty-nine percent) prefer watching the news on TV, and thirty-five percent regularly log on to news websites. Thirty-one percent of you read or listen to the news every day, but only sixteen percent like watching current affairs shows. You're more interested in national news than international news, but nearly eighty-five percent of our readers watch news flashes about important events in the world.

So, is there any room for newspapers in today's world? Twenty-three percent of you said yes, but more than half (fifty-one percent) said you could live without them. Jake and Lisa explain their views:

Jake Moreno (16)
I've never bought a newspaper. I usually find out about the news through a social networking site. That's how I heard about the tsunami in Japan. One of my friends added a link to a news flash. News websites are good too, because you can listen to podcasts and watch videos.

Lisa Sherman (15)
I sometimes look at news websites, but I haven't had time this week (too much homework!). I usually read a newspaper on the school bus. I follow the local news, and I also read the sports section.

Grammar • Present perfect

Affirmative
I/You/We/They have ('ve) read the news.
He/She/It has ('s) read the news.

Negative
I/You/We/They have not (haven't) read the news.
He/She/It has not (hasn't) read the news.

Questions and short answers
Have I/you/we/they heard the news?
Yes, I/you/we/they have. / No, I/you/we/they haven't.
Has he/she/it heard the news?
Yes, he/she/it has. / No, he/she/it hasn't.

Watch Out!
Have you ever bought a newspaper?
He has never bought a newspaper.

Grammar reference Workbook page 92

1 Study the grammar table and Watch Out! Complete the rules with these words.

> an unspecified past time   ever   have/has   never

1 We use the Present perfect to talk about an experience that happened at …. , but is relevant to the present.
2 We make the Present perfect with …. and the Past participle.
3 We use …. to ask about experiences.
4 We use …. to talk about experiences we haven't had.

2 Complete the sentences with the Present perfect form of these verbs.

> buy   ~~not buy~~   not finish
> not go   not hear   write

1 Sorry, I *haven't bought* a newspaper. I haven't had time!
2 My sister is a journalist. She …. a lot of articles.
3 I can't go out tonight. I …. my homework.
4 He …. finally … a new cell phone.
5 They …. to the beach. It's too cold!
6 I …. the final score of the game. Did we win?

3 Complete the conversation. Then listen and check.
2.3
Girl ¹ *Have* you *seen* (see) the new school website?
Boy   No, I ² …. . Is it good?
Girl It's great! It has school news, movie reviews and jokes on it.
Boy   What about football? ³ …. the PE teacher …. (write) about our school team's last game?
Girl No, he ⁴ …. . Why don't you write about it?
Boy   I don't know how to write a report. ⁵ …. you …. (ever/do) something like that?
Girl Yes, I ⁶ …. . I ⁷ …. (write) about school uniforms for the school newspaper before, and I ⁸ …. (interview) some teachers. You should interview the principal.
Boy   No way! I ⁹ …. (not interview) anyone before!
Girl Well, listen to mine first. They ¹⁰ …. (put) a podcast of my interviews on the website.

4 Complete the questions and answers.

1 A *Have you ever been* (you/ever/be) to the US?
  B Yes, I have.
2 A …. (you/ever/meet) a famous person?
  B No, I …. (never/meet) a famous person.
3 A …. (you/ever/play) basketball?
  B Yes, I …. .
4 A …. (he/ever/write) a blog?
  B No, he …. (never/write) a blog.
5 A …. (she/ever/be) late for school?
  B Yes, she …. !
6 A …. (they/ever/buy) a computer game?
  B Yes, they …. .

5 What about you? In pairs, ask and answer.

Have you ever …
• go to a rock concert?
• wear red sneakers?
• try skateboarding?
• see a horror movie?
• have a pet?
• write a poem?
• be on TV?
• stand on your head?

Have you ever been to a rock concert?

Yes, I have. It was fantastic!

Unit 4 • In the News

Vocabulary • Adverbs of manner

1 Look at these words. Check the meaning in a dictionary. Listen and repeat.
2.4

angrily	badly	carefully	carelessly	early
fast	happily	hard	late	loudly
patiently	quietly	sadly	slowly	~~well~~

Word list page 77
Workbook page 107

2 Complete the sentences with the words in Exercise 1.
1 He's a good journalist. He writes very *well*.
2 She's a hard worker. She works very …. .
3 He felt sad for me. He looked at me …. .
4 They were late for the party. They arrived …. .
5 He's very quiet. He speaks …. , too.
6 The politician was angry. He answered the questions …. .
7 They're slow readers. They read …. .
8 He's so careless. He does things …. .

3 Choose the correct options to complete the text.

How to Be a News Anchor

TV news anchors work very ¹ *hard / badly*. I get up very ² *early / late* every day, around 5 a.m. When I get to the TV studio, there's a lot of information to read. I read it ³ *slowly / fast* so I know the main stories. I read it again later to get more detail. Then a hairstylist does my hair, and I choose my clothes ⁴ *carefully / carelessly*. You can't wear black, white or red—cameras have problems with these colors!
I'm always ready early, but I wait ⁵ *angrily / patiently* for the show to start. Then I smile ⁶ *sadly / happily* and read the news headlines. I speak clearly (but not too ⁷ *quietly / loudly*), so people can understand what I say. It's an interesting job, and I do it ⁸ *badly / well*!

4 Correct the sentences. Use these words.

| badly | carefully | fast |
| happily | ~~loudly~~ | patiently |

1 The class sang **quietly**. It was really noisy. *loudly*
2 Jamal spent a long time taking the photo. He did it very **carelessly**.
3 Jasmin smiled **sadly** when she won first prize.
4 We ran very **slowly**. We were late for school!
5 Kevin did **well** on his exams. He didn't get good grades.
6 The teacher explained the homework **angrily**. He wanted everyone to understand.

5 What about you? In pairs, ask and answer.
1 Do you work slowly or fast?
2 Do you get to school early or late?
3 Do you work hard in class?
4 Do you usually play your music loudly or quietly?
5 Do you do usually do well or badly on school exams?

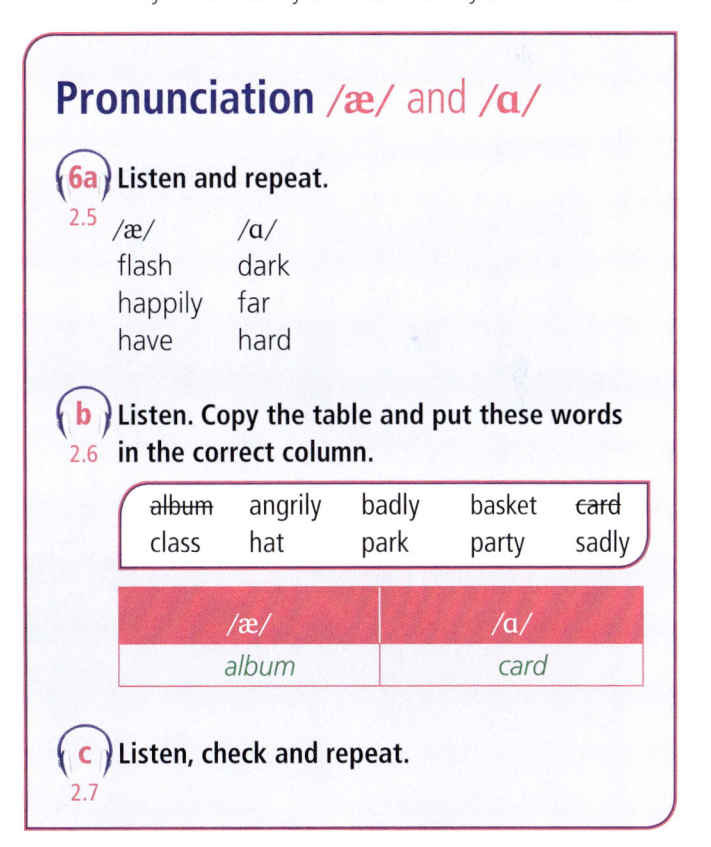

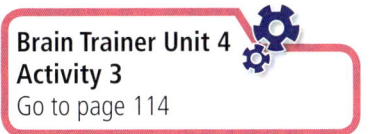

Pronunciation /æ/ and /ɑ/

6a Listen and repeat.
2.5

/æ/	/ɑ/
flash	dark
happily	far
have	hard

b Listen. Copy the table and put these words
2.6 in the correct column.

| ~~album~~ | angrily | badly | basket | ~~card~~ |
| class | hat | park | party | sadly |

/æ/	/ɑ/
album	card

c Listen, check and repeat.
2.7

Brain Trainer Unit 4
Activity 3
Go to page 114

Unit 4 • In the News

Chatroom Doubt and disbelief

Speaking and Listening

1 Look at the photo. Answer the questions.
1. Where are the teenagers?
2. What are they doing?
3. What do you think has happened?

2 Listen and read the conversation.
2.8 Check your answers.

3 Listen and read again. Answer
2.8 the questions.
1. What escaped from the zoo?
   A snake.
2. Where did they find it?
3. Who found it?
4. What did she think it was?
5. What was probably terrified?
6. Who isn't scared of snakes?

4 Act out the conversation in groups of four.

Tom Hey, have you heard the story about the snake?
Ash What snake?
Tom The snake from the zoo. It escaped last week. Well, they have found it.
Ash Oh yeah? Where?
Tom In a store in town.
Ash No! Really?
Tom Yes, listen to this: "Carrie James, a local teenager, found the snake when she was shopping in Trend clothing store yesterday."
Ella I don't believe it! I shop there all the time.
Tom "I thought it was a scarf," said Carrie, "but when I touched it, it moved away quickly."
Ash That's ridiculous!
Tom It gets better. "I've never touched a snake before," said Carrie. "I'm glad I didn't try it on!"
Ella Ugh! Imagine that!
Ruby Poor snake! It was probably terrified.
Ella Poor snake? You're kidding!
Ruby No, I'm not. I really like snakes.

Say it in your language …
It gets better.
Imagine that!

48 Unit 4 • In the News

5 Look back at the conversation. Who says what?

1 No! Really? *Ash*
2 I don't believe it!
3 That's ridiculous!
4 You're kidding!

6 Read the phrases for expressing doubt and disbelief.

Expressing doubt and disbelief
No! Really?
I don't believe it.
That's strange.
That's impossible.
You're kidding!
That's ridiculous!

7 Listen to the conversations. Act out
2.9 the conversations in pairs.

Ruby I met [1] Justin Bieber in LA last week.
Tom   I don't believe it.
Ruby But it's true!

Ella [2] Our school was on TV yesterday.
Ruby That's impossible!
Ella No, it isn't. Take a look at [3] the news website.

Tom   I put [4] a video of my dog online.
Ash   You're kidding!
Tom   No, I'm not. Here it is.

8 Work in pairs. Replace the words in purple in Exercise 7. Use these words and/or your own ideas. Act out the conversations.

> I met our principal in the café yesterday.

> I don't believe it.

1 Lady Gaga in New York / Angelina Jolie in Hollywood / LeBron James in Miami

2 my best friend / my dad / my brother

3 the local news / my blog

4 a photo of my party / a video of my cat / a picture of me in my Superman costume

Grammar • Present perfect vs Past simple

Present perfect	Past simple
A snake has escaped from the zoo.	A snake escaped from the zoo last week.
I've never touched a snake before.	She didn't touch the snake.
Have they found the snake?	A teenager found the snake in a store yesterday.

Grammar reference Workbook page 92

1 Study the grammar table. Choose the correct options to complete the rules.

1 We use the *Past simple / Present perfect* to talk about something that happened at an unspecified time in the past, but is relevant to the present.
2 We use the *Past simple / Present perfect* to talk about something that happened at a specific time in the past.

2 Complete the sentences with the Past simple or Present perfect form of the verbs.

1 finish
  a OK, I *'ve finished* my homework. Can I watch TV?
  b I *finished* my homework half an hour ago.
2 eat
  a .... you all .... dinner yet?
  b We .... all the pizza last night.
3 lose
  a I .... my glasses at the mall last weekend.
  b I .... my glasses again. I really need them!

3 Make conversations.

A you ever / meet a famous person?
  Have you ever met a famous person?
B Yes, I have.
A Really? Who / you / meet?
B I / meet Keira Knightley last year.

A you / ever go / to a skatepark?
B Yes, I have.
A When / you / go?
B I / go / to one last week.

Unit 4 • In the News

Reading

1 Look at the photo. Answer the questions.

1 What do you think the woman's job is?
2 How would you describe her work?
- dangerous
- safe
- boring
- interesting
- easy
- difficult

Teen News

Profile: Christiane Amanpour

Christiane Amanpour is small with dark hair. She looks like an ordinary person, but she is one of the world's most famous journalists.

Christiane was born in England in 1958 and went to school
5 there and in Iran. She studied journalism in the US, and when she graduated from college, she got a job as an assistant with CNN. "I arrived at CNN with a suitcase, my bicycle and 100 dollars," she says. It was a difficult introduction to journalism, but Christiane worked hard, and she soon
10 became a foreign correspondent.

Life as a foreign correspondent is busy and often dangerous. They fly to different countries and report on international news there. Their reports appear on news websites, in newspapers and on TV, and thousands—
15 sometimes millions—of people see them.

Christiane has been all over the world and reported on many different stories. Some of them are the biggest stories of the twentieth century. She has reported on wars and natural disasters, and she has also interviewed world
20 leaders and politicians. She has often been in danger, but luckily she has never been injured. Christiane won the Courage in Journalism Award in 1994 for her war reports, but she is modest about it. "It's our job to go to these places and bring back stories, just as a window on the
25 world," she says.

Today Christiane anchors an international news show called *Amanpour*. She interviews people in a TV studio, so she doesn't travel much, but she still tells people what is happening in the world. "I believe that good journalism,
30 good television, can make our world a better place," she says.

Key Words

foreign correspondent   wars
natural disasters   world leaders
politicians   modest

2 Read the magazine article and check your answers to Exercise 1.

3 Read the article again. Answer the questions.
2.10
1 Why is Christiane Amanpour special?
She is one of the world's most famous journalists.
2 Where did she study journalism?
3 What was her first job?
4 What do foreign correspondents do?
5 Why did Christiane win the Courage in Journalism Award?
6 What does she do now?

4 What do these words refer to?
1 there (line 5) *in England*
2 she (line 9)
3 them (line 15)
4 them (line 17)
5 it (line 23)

Listening

1 Look at these opinions about the news.
2.11 Which do you agree with?

a I'm not interested in international news.

b The news is usually bad. It's often about wars or natural disasters.

c It's good to know what is happening in the world.

Listening Bank Unit 4 page 118

2 Think about a story in the news this week. Answer the questions.
1 Is it national, international or local news?
2 Where did you see it?
3 What is the story about?

Writing • A profile

1 Read the Writing File.

> **Writing File**   Error correction
>
> When you have finished your writing, always check:
> - spelling
> - punctuation
> - grammar
>
> Then write your final draft.

2 Read the profile. Find and correct six errors.
- two punctuation
- two spelling
- two grammar

1 *canterbury – Canterbury*

Profile: Orlando Bloom

Orlando Bloom is a great actor and is often in the newspapers, but I admire him because of his work for UNICEF *.

Orlando was born in 1977 in a town called canterbury. He has gone to school there with his sister, Samantha. Reading and riting weren't easy for Orlando, but he always wanted to be an actor After school, he studied drama in London, then he got the part of Legolas in *The Lord of the Rings*.

Today Orlando was very famous, but he's used his fame to help other people. He has visited schools and villages in Nepal and has helped to support clean water and education progams there. Orlando Bloom is not just a pretty face, he cares about people and the world around him. That's why I admire him.

* UNICEF is the United Nations children's charity.

3 Look at these sentences about the actor, Orlando Bloom. Find and correct the errors. (S = spelling, G = grammar, P = punctuation)

1 Orlando Bloom is ofen in the newspapers. (S)   *often*
2 His most exiting movie is *Pirates of the Caribbean*. (S)
3 When he was 15, he has gotten a tattoo. (G)
4 He broke his nose while he is playing rugby. (G)
5 He has a dog named sidi. (P)
6 Is he working in Hollywood now. (P)

4 Read the profile again. Answer the questions.

1 Who did Orlando go to school with?
   His sister, Samantha
2 What did Orlando always want to be?
3 Where did he study drama?
4 How has he helped other people?
5 Why does the writer admire Orlando Bloom?

5 Think about a famous person who you admire. Answer these questions. Take notes.

1 Why is he/she famous?
2 Why do you admire him/her?
3 When was he/she born?
4 Where did he/she go to school?
5 What does he/she do today?

6 Write a profile of the person you chose in Exercise 5. Use "My famous person" and your notes from Exercise 5.

> **My famous person**
>
> **Paragraph 1**
> Introduction and why you admire him/her
> …. (name) *is a great* …. (job). *I admire him/her because of his/her* …. .
>
> **Paragraph 2**
> Early life, education and career
> …. *was born in* …. (when?) *in* …. (where?). *After school, he/she* …. (what did he/she do?)
>
> **Paragraph 3**
> What he/she has done recently and why you admire him/her
> *Today* …. (name) *is* …. (describe him/her). *He/She has* …. (what has he/she done?)

Remember!
- Use the vocabulary from this and earlier units where possible.
- Check your grammar, spelling and punctuation.

Refresh Your Memory!

Grammar • Review

1 Complete the text about a famous reporter. Use the Present perfect form of the verbs.

Clark Kent works for the *Daily Planet*. He's tired because he ¹ *'s had* (have) a busy day. What ² …. he …. (do)? Well, he ³ …. (meet) the mayor of Metropolis, and he ⁴ …. (write) a report for the newspaper. He ⁵ …. (work) with his friend Lois on a big story. They ⁶ …. (not finish) it because they ⁷ …. (not interview) Lex Luthor. Clark ⁸ …. (not see) Lex today, but he ⁹ …. (fly) around the city and helped people. Clark Kent has two jobs. ¹⁰ …. you …. (ever/hear) of Superman?

2 Make sentences and questions.

1 you / ever / read / a newspaper on the bus?
Have you ever read a newspaper on the bus?
2 I / never / play / ice hockey
3 they / ever / watch / a video online?
4 He / never / act / in a movie
5 she / ever / interview / a pop star?
6 We / never / try / playing rugby

3 Choose the correct options.

1 Some teenagers *have never bought* / *never bought* a newspaper.
2 Mike *has read* / *read* an interesting blog about computer games last night.
3 There *has been* / *was* a news flash about a tsunami this morning.
4 She *has never eaten* / *didn't eat* at a pizza place. She doesn't like pizza.
5 We *haven't seen* / *didn't see* the football game last weekend.

Vocabulary • Review

4 Read the definitions and complete the words.

1 You can listen to this on your MP3 player. p<u>odc</u>a<u>st</u>
2 This person often writes for a newspaper. j_ _rn_l_st
3 The most important news stories are the h_ _dl_n_s.
4 Important new stories usually appear in a n_ws fl_sh on TV.
5 People use this to write about their everyday lives. bl_g
6 On a computer, we can read the news on a n_ws w_bs_t_.

5 Complete the sentences with the correct adverb form of the adjective in parentheses.

1 The actor is smiling *happily* (happy) in the photo.
2 My brother is playing his music very …. (loud).
3 Saul always does his homework very …. (careful).
4 I play tennis really …. (bad).
5 The reporter waited …. (patient) for his first interview to begin.
6 The bus doesn't go very …. (fast), but it's cheaper than the train.

Speaking • Review

6 Complete the conversation with these words. Then listen and check. (2.12)

| happen | headlines | ~~heard~~ | impossible | kidding |

Girl Have you ¹ *heard* the news? An elephant has escaped from the zoo.
Boy That's ² …. !
Girl No, it isn't. Look at the ³ …. . I'm not ⁴ …. .
Boy Wow! It *is* true. That's ridiculous!
Girl I know, but how did it ⁵ …. ?

Dictation

7 Listen and write in your notebook. (2.13)

✓ My assessment profile: Workbook page 130

Real World Profiles

Tavi Gevinson's Profile

Age
14 years old

Home country
United States

My favorite things …
fashion, writing (check out my fashion blog and Internet magazine for teenage girls), art

Tavi Gevinson: Writer and Magazine Editor

Tavi Gevinson was born in 1996. She has two older sisters and lives with her family in Oak Park, Illinois. She just graduated from high school and is planning to go to college.

When Tavi was a child, she became interested in fashion and art, and began to explore fashion blogs and magazines. She wanted to present her personal style to other people and talk about trends in fashion. So she started writing her own blog when she was only eleven years old. The blog became popular very fast, and Tavi attended New York Fashion Week and gave interviews in several magazines.

At the age of sixteen, Tavi started her second website, *Rookie*, which is an online magazine for teenage girls (www.rookiemag.com). She explains, "I just felt like there wasn't really anything … that was honest … to an audience of teenage girls or respected their intelligence." The online magazine helps teenage girls to connect with each other and share their experiences. It covers a different theme each month, like "The Great Unknown" or "Together," and is updated three times a day. Many teenage girls contribute their writing, photographs, illustrations or videos to the website. The magazine talks about different cultural and political topics that are important to teenagers today. Tavi works as the magazine's editor-in-chief, and she has edited print versions of the best content from the website, called *Rookie Yearbook*.

Tavi is much busier than most teenagers. She works very hard on her magazine and travels a lot. But she is happy to be part of *Rookie*. "It's a job. … And I'm OK with that, 'cause it's something that I care about," she says.

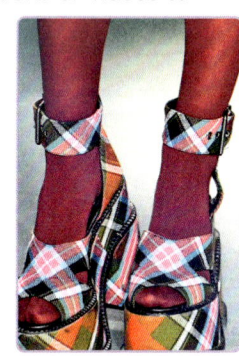

Key Words
magazine, contribute, theme, editor, connect, content

Reading

1 Read Tavi's profile. Are the statements true (T) or false (F)?

1 Tavi is from the US. T
2 She likes sports.
3 She has an online magazine.
4 The magazine is for adult women.

2 Read the article. Answer the questions.
2.14
1 How old was Tavi when she started her fashion blog?
She was eleven.
2 What did Tavi start at age sixteen?
3 How often is Tavi's online magazine updated?
4 What topics does the magazine cover?
5 What makes Tavi different from other teenagers?

Class discussion

1 Do you read any blogs on the Internet? What are they about?
2 Would you write about your personal life online? Why?/Why not?
3 Do you feel that the Internet connects teenagers or makes them more lonely?

5 Enjoy Your Vacation!

Grammar
Present perfect + *for* and *since*; *How long?*; Past simple with *just*

Vocabulary
- Vacation;
- Meanings of *get*

Speaking
Asking for information

Writing
A travel guide

Word list page 77
Workbook page 108

Vocabulary • Vacation

1 Match the pictures (1–14) to these activities. Then listen, check and repeat.
2.15

book a flight/hotel 1	buy souvenirs	check into a hotel	eat out
get a tan	get lost	go camping	go sightseeing
lose your luggage	pack your bag	put up a tent	stay in a hotel
take a trip	write a travel blog		

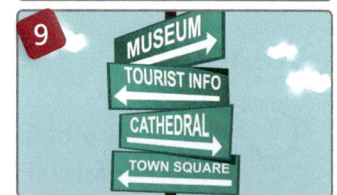

2 Match the sentences to the activities in Exercise 1.

1 We have flights and we've paid for the hotel— I think that's everything. *book a flight/hotel*
2 All the other bags came off the plane, but mine wasn't there!
3 This pink T-shirt is great. It says "I Love NY."
4 I've almost finished, but the bag is really heavy!
5 I want to see the famous cathedral.
6 Let's go to the restaurant by the beach tonight!
7 I'm not sure how to get back to the hotel!

3 Match the verbs (1–6) to the nouns (a–f) to make activities from Exercise 1.

1 stay   a into a hotel
2 write   b a tan
3 go   c a tent
4 check   d a travel blog
5 get   e in a hotel
6 put up   f camping

4 What about you? In pairs, ask and answer.

1 Where do you usually stay when you go on vacation?
2 What do you enjoy doing? Do you like getting a tan or going sightseeing?
3 Have you ever written a travel blog?

I usually stay in a hotel.

Brain Trainer Unit 5
Activity 2
Go to page 114

54 Unit 5 • Enjoy Your Vacation!

Reading

1 Look at the photos from Shannon and Jenna's vacation. Answer the questions.

1 What type of vacation is it?
2 Where do you think they are staying?
3 What do you think they do every day?

2 Read the magazine article quickly and check your answers to Exercise 1. Which activity in the photos have Shannon and Jenna not done?

3 Read the article again. Answer the questions.

2.16 Who …
1 likes staying in hotels? *Shannon*
2 likes doing different activities?
3 has never planned a vacation before?
4 has never stayed in a tent before?
5 usually reads books on vacation?
6 has enjoyed the vacation?

4 What about you? In pairs, ask and answer.

1 What do your parents like to do on vacation? Do you like the same things or different things?
2 What are the advantages of a family vacation? Are there any disadvantages?

Advantages
Stay in a nice hotel.
Parents pay for everything.

Disadvantages
Can't stay up late.
Difficult to meet other teenagers.

BEHIND THE CAMERA

People have different ideas about what makes a good vacation, especially parents and their children. In a new TV show, *You Choose!*, kids decide on the family vacation, with some funny results! This week, 16-year-old Jenna Roberts packs the bags and chooses the destination. Her mom, Shannon, gets a big surprise. We asked them about their experiences.

"I think Mom liked canoeing …"

Jenna's story

Mom has always decided where to go on vacation since I was little. We usually stay in hotels, and Mom just likes getting a tan or she reads books all day. I don't mind swimming or listening to my MP3 player, but I like adventure too, so I chose a vacation at the lake. No hotels, no swimming pools, just a tent in a campground (Mom has never put up a tent before). How long have we been here? Mom says "forever!," but actually we've been here for five days. We've tried mountain biking, rock climbing and canoeing since last weekend. Mom was scared on the rock climb, but I think she liked canoeing …

Shannon's story

I was worried when Jenna chose our vacation. I like to relax and read when I'm away, but Jenna is really active. She gets bored easily. It hasn't been a great vacation because I haven't read a book since Saturday. In fact, I haven't read anything for a whole week, but I've had some time to talk to Jenna. That's been the best part, really. We're both too busy to talk at home!

Grammar • Present perfect + *for* and *since*; *How long*?

How long have we been here?
We've been here for five days/a week/a month.

I haven't read a book since Saturday.

She's lived in Philadelphia since 2010.

Grammar reference Workbook page 94

1 Study the grammar table. Choose the correct options to complete the rules.

1 We use *for / since* with a period of time.

2 We use *for / since* with a point in time.

2 Copy the table and put these words and phrases in the correct column.

a long time	August	a week
five o'clock	four years	I was fifteen
last week	last weekend	ten minutes
Tuesday	two days	yesterday

for	since
a long time	August

3 Make sentences with the Present perfect. Add *for* or *since* to each sentence.

1 They / be on / vacation / weeks
   They have been on vacation for weeks.
2 You / be on my game console / hours!
3 He / not watch TV / last weekend
4 We / stay in the same hotel / the last two weeks
5 I / not write my travel blog / a long time
6 We / eat local food / we arrived
7 They / not see their friends / Friday

4 Complete the text about an unusual vacation. Use the verbs and choose *for* or *since*.

Jill Daniels ¹ *has had* (have) a new bike ² *for / since* Christmas. When she got her bike, she went on a biking trip. She ³ .... (be) on her trip ⁴ *for / since* three months now, and she ⁵ .... (travel) thousands of kilometers. She ⁶ .... (visit) six different countries, and she ⁷ .... (be) in Portugal ⁸ *for / since* Thursday. However, she ⁹ .... (not stay) in a hotel or put up a tent ¹⁰ *for / since* December. Why? Because Jill's bike ¹¹ .... (not leave) her house! "It's a virtual vacation on an exercise bike," explains Jill. "I bike 20 kilometers every day. I haven't gotten a tan, and I ¹² .... (not buy) any souvenirs, but I'm enjoying it!"

5 Make questions and answers about Exercise 4.

1 How long / Jill / had a new bike?
   How long has Jill had a new bike? Since Christmas.
2 How long / she / be on her trip?
3 How long / she / be in Portugal?
4 How many kilometers / she / travel?
5 How many countries / she visit?

Pronunciation /aɪ/ vs /ɪ/

6a Listen and repeat.
2.17

| active | arrive | bike | give | I've | like |
| live | sign | miss | since | time | visit |

b Copy the table and put the words in Exercise 6a in the correct column.

/aɪ/	/ɪ/
arrive	active

c Listen, check and repeat.
2.18

7 What about you? In pairs, ask and answer.

1 How long have you lived in your town/city?
2 How long have you had a cell phone?
3 How long have you known your best friend?

How long have you lived in your town?

I've lived here for ten years.

Unit 5 • Enjoy Your Vacation!

Vocabulary • Meanings of *get*

1 Match the pictures (1–6) to the different meanings of the verb *get* (a–f).

a It was dark when we got to the campsite.
   = arrive
b Damian got a key ring and a baseball cap from the souvenir shop. = buy 1
c We got their postcard after they arrived home from their vacation. = receive
d Can you get the bottle of sunscreen from our hotel room? = bring
e It was getting cold on the beach, so we went home. = become
f He got on the bus and bought a ticket.
   = walk/move

Word list page 77
Workbook page 108

2 Read the sentences. Replace *get* with one of these verbs in the correct form.

arrive   become   buy   bring   receive   walk

1 Hurry up! We won't get to school on time!
  Hurry up! We won't arrive at school on time!
2 I think adventure vacations are getting more dangerous.
3 When you book a flight online, you get the tickets in an email.
4 She got a lot of new clothes for her vacation.
5 Can you get the guidebook? I left it in my bag.
6 Someone checked our passports before we got onto the plane.

3 What would you say in these situations? Make a question or a sentence with *get*.

1 You like your friend's new bag. You want to know where she bought it.
  Where did you get your bag?
2 You sent your friend a text message. You want to know if he received it.
  Did you …. ?
3 You see your friends at a party. You ask them what time they arrived.
  When …. ?
4 You are at a train station with a friend. Your train has arrived.
  Come on. Let's …. .
5 Your mother has left her jacket upstairs. You offer to bring it to her.
  Don't worry. I'll …. .

4 **What about you?** In pairs, ask and answer.

1 How many text messages do you get a day?
2 What time do you usually get to school?
3 What things can you do to get healthy?
4 How often do you get on a bus to go to school?

> How many text messages do you get a day?

> I get about twenty text messages a day.

**Brain Trainer Unit 5
Activity 3**
Go to page 115

Unit 5 • Enjoy Your Vacation!

Chatroom Asking for information

Speaking and Listening

1 Look at the photo. Answer the questions.
1. Where do you think they have been?
2. What are they doing?
3. What do you think Tom's dad is asking?

2 Listen and read the conversation.
2.19 Check your answers.

3 Listen and read again. Answer the questions.
2.19
1. Who liked the souvenir shops? *Tom*
2. What does Ash want to do?
3. Where does Tom want to go next?
4. How does the girl help them?
5. How can they get there?
6. What does Ash want to know?

4 Act out the conversation in groups of four.

Mr. Green	What did you think of Brighton Pier, boys?
Tom	I really liked the souvenir shops.
Ash	The cafés were nice, too. Can we have lunch soon?
Tom	You just had ice cream, Ash! Let's go see Brighton Pavilion first.
Ash	Is it far?
Mr. Green	Let's ask someone. Excuse me. Can you help us? We want to get to Brighton Pavilion.
Girl	Sure. Let me show you on the map. You're here … and Brighton Pavilion is there. You can't miss it.
Mr. Green	How can we get there?
Girl	Well, you just missed the bus, but it's only a ten-minute walk.
Ash	Is there a good place to eat there?
Girl	Oh yes! There's a really good restaurant there. The menu just changed, and the food's delicious.
Ash	Thank goodness. I'm starving!

Say it in your language …
Thank goodness. I'm starving!

Unit 5 • Enjoy Your Vacation!

5 Look back at the conversation. Who says what?

1 Is it far? *Ash*
2 Excuse me. Can you help us?
3 How can we get there?
4 Is there a good place to eat there?

6 Read the phrases for asking for information.

Asking for information
Excuse me. Can you help us/me?
Where's a good place to …?
Is there a good place to … there?
How can we/I get there?
Is it far?
How long does it take to get to …?

7 Listen to the conversations. What information
2.20 do the people ask for? Act out the conversations in pairs.

Ash   Excuse me. Can you help us? Where's a good place to ¹ eat out?
Girl There's a ² pizza place near the beach.
Ash   Thanks. That's great.
Tom   Excuse me. Can you help me?
Girl Sure.
Tom   Where's a good place to ¹ buy souvenirs?
Girl There's a ² great shop in the Brighton Pavilion.
Tom   Is it far?
Girl ³ No. It's only a five-minute walk.

8 Work in pairs. Replace the words in purple in Exercise 7. Use these words and/or your own ideas. Act out the conversations.

> Excuse me. Can you help us? Where's a good place to buy a map?

> There's a newsstand near the station.

1 buy clothes / have a drink / go swimming

2 good store in the mall / café near the pier / swimming pool near the park

3 No. It's about five minutes by bus. / Yes. It's about a twenty-minute walk. / No. It's right there.

Grammar • Past simple with *just*

You *just* had ice cream.
You *just* missed the bus.
The menu *just* changed.

Grammar reference Workbook page 94

1 Study the grammar table. Choose the correct option to complete the rule.

The Past simple with *just* describes an action that happened *a short time ago* / *a long time ago*.

2 Make sentences with *just*.

1 He / get a hamburger and fries
  He just got a hamburger and fries.
2 I / get a postcard from my friend
3 She / go for a swim
4 We / pack our bags
5 He / buy some souvenirs
6 I / find the guidebook
7 They / check into their hotel

3 In pairs, say what just happened. Use the ideas below.

book a hotel	his brother/tell a joke
leave the house	lose their luggage
put up a tent	start their homework
their team/win a game	

1 He's excited.
2 They're worried.
3 We're tired.
4 He's laughing.
5 She isn't home.
6 They're happy.
7 You're bored.

> Why is he excited?

> He just booked a hotel.

Reading

1 Look at the photos of these tourist attractions. Which would you like to visit? Why?

Strange Tourist Attractions

This week in *Vacation Vistas* you can read about tourist attractions with a difference.

Bubble Gum Alley, San Luis Obispo, California, US
In 1950, this was just a normal passage between buildings. Then students from two local schools started to leave their bubble gum on its walls. They wrote messages with the gum and made pictures. Some people loved the bubble gum in the alley, but others hated it, and local store owners cleaned it a few times. But the students and their bubble gum always came back.

Today the alley is called Bubble Gum Alley, and it is still full of gum. Students leave most of it, but tourists and artists leave gum, too. Artist Matthew Hoffman recently made a big picture of a man blowing a bubble! "It's fantastic!" says one visitor. "Disgusting!" says another. What do *you* think?

Upside Down House, Szymbark, Poland
Daniel Czapiewski built this house in 2007, and thousands of tourists have visited it since then. He built it because he thinks many things in the world are wrong—upside down—and his house is a symbol of this.

You usually enter a house through the door, but to get into the Upside Down House, you climb through a window. When you are inside, you walk along the ceiling, go under a table and look up at a bed. In the bathroom, there's a toilet on the ceiling; in the living room there's an upside down TV.

Inside the house, there's an art exhibition. It's called "Let's Save This World," and the pictures show different world problems. Czapiewski wants people to think about these things. "I just visited the house, and I like its message," said one tourist, "but it made me feel dizzy!"

Key Words

tourist attractions	passage
bubble gum	blowing a bubble
upside down	dizzy

2 Read the magazine article. Match the statements
2.21 to the attractions. (A = Bubble Gum Alley, B = Upside Down House)

1 Some people don't like it. *A*
2 Furniture is in the wrong place.
3 It's popular with students.
4 It has something important to say.
5 You can walk along it.
6 You feel confused inside.
7 You can see serious pictures there.
8 You can see a funny picture there.

3 Read the article again. Are the statements true (T) or false (F)?

1 The first people to leave bubble gum in the alley were artists. *F*
2 Some people tried to clean the walls in the alley.
3 Everybody loves Bubble Gum Alley.
4 The Upside Down House represents what the artist thinks is wrong with the world.
5 You go into the house through a window.
6 The TV is in the living room.

Listening

1 Listen to the radio interview. Then complete
2.22 the sentence.

The most unusual place Troy has ever stayed in is in .... .

Listening Bank Unit 5 page 119

2 Think about a tourist attraction in your country.

1 Where is it?
2 What is it?
3 What is it like? Describe it.
4 How long has it been a tourist attraction?
5 Who visits the place and why? What do people think of it?

Unit 5 • Enjoy Your Vacation!

Writing • A travel guide

1 Read the Writing File.

> **Writing File** Making your writing more interesting
>
> - Use different adjectives to make your writing more interesting.
> - Use new vocabulary you have learned, too. It's a good way to remember new words!

2 Read the travel guide. Find the opposites of these adjectives.

1. large *small*
2. unfriendly
3. rainy
4. ugly
5. unknown
6. terrible

3 Find the adjectives in these sentences. Then copy and complete the table.

1. San Francisco is a big city, and it's very busy.
2. The most popular attraction is the Golden Gate Bridge.
3. There's an interesting museum and a famous park, too.
4. People are usually helpful and friendly.
5. The weather is often foggy and cold.

Town/City	*big, busy*
People	
Weather	
Tourist attractions	

4 Read the travel guide again. Answer the questions.

1. Where is Brighton? *It's in southern England.*
2. What are the people like there?
3. What is the weather like?
4. What are the main attractions?
5. How can you find out what's happening in Brighton?

5 Think about your town or city. Answer the questions. Take notes.

1. Where is it?
2. What do you think of it?
3. What are the people like?
4. Is the weather usually good or bad?
5. Are there any famous tourist attractions?
6. What activities can you do there?

6 Write a travel guide. Use "My favorite town/city" and your notes from Exercise 5.

> **My favorite town/city**
>
> 1. Introduce your town/city.
> 2. Describe what you can see and do.
> 3. Give your conclusion.

Travel Guide: My City by Hayley West

My hometown is Brighton. It's a small city, near the sea, in southern England. I love living in Brighton because the people are friendly, and the weather is usually sunny. There are also a lot of music festivals here.

There are many things to see and do in Brighton. One of the main attractions is Brighton Pavilion. It's a beautiful palace, and it's more than two hundred years old! Another famous attraction is Brighton Pier. There's a fantastic amusement park there. You can also sit in a beach café or buy some souvenirs. If you enjoy watersports, you can go windsurfing or sailing, too.

Brighton is a great city and has a lot to offer. When you visit Brighton, get a newspaper and see what's going on. You might get a nice surprise!

> **Remember!**
> - Use different adjectives to make your writing more interesting.
> - Use the vocabulary in this unit.
> - Check your grammar, spelling and punctuation.

Refresh Your Memory!

Grammar • Review

1 Match the beginnings (1–8) to the endings (a–h) of the sentences.

1 They've been on vacation for *b*
2 He's lived in southern California since
3 I waited two hours for
4 She hasn't written her travel blog for
5 I haven't worn a T-shirt since
6 We've tried a lot of different sports since
7 They haven't had a sunny day for
8 I haven't received a text message since

a a long time. She has a lot to write about.
b three weeks. They don't want to go home.
c he was a child. He speaks fluent Spanish.
d weeks. It's been very cloudy.
e last weekend. I miss my friends!
f we arrived. We've been really busy!
g a train this morning. I was fed up.
h Monday. It's been too cold!

2 Complete the sentences. Use *just* and these verbs.

| arrive | buy | eat | ~~finish~~ |
| get | have | miss | pass |

1 Sorry, there isn't any more pizza. We *just finished* it.
2 They .... some souvenirs. They don't have any more money.
3 That was the mail carrier. I .... a letter.
4 He's very tired. He .... home.
5 She's upset. She .... an argument with her mother.
6 I .... my exam. I'm very happy!
7 We .... the last bus. We'll have to walk home.
8 I .... the last slice of bread. I'll have to go to the supermarket later.

Vocabulary • Review

3 Complete the sentences with these verbs.

| buy | get | packed | ~~put up~~ | stay | went | write |

1 We arrived at the campsite, *put up* our tent, then made a pot of coffee.
2 Have you .... your bag? Yes, I'm ready to go.
3 I sometimes .... a travel blog on vacation.
4 If we take a map with us, we won't .... lost.
5 He doesn't .... souvenirs on vacation because he never has enough money.
6 We usually .... in a five-star hotel, but this year we .... camping.

4 Match the meanings of *get* (a–f) to the sentences (1–6).

a arrive *2*
b buy
c receive
d bring
e become
f walk/move

1 I **got** your text message this morning. What's the matter?
2 I was late for school this morning. I **got** there at nine thirty!
3 Can you **get** the basketball? It's in the car.
4 He **got** a new computer game with his birthday money.
5 School exams **are getting** more difficult.
6 When the school bus arrived, we all **got** on.

Speaking • Review

5 Put the conversation in the correct order. Then listen and check.
2.23

a No. It's only a five-minute walk.
b Excuse me. Can you help me? *1*
c There's a good souvenir shop on Cedar Street.
d Where's a good place to buy postcards?
e Sure.
f Is it far?

Dictation

6 Listen and write in your notebook.
2.24

✓ **My assessment profile:** Workbook page 131

62 Unit 5 • Enjoy Your Vacation!

Literature File

Gulliver's Travels
by Jonathan Swift

Introduction
It's 1726 and Gulliver is traveling across the ocean from England. There's a storm, and his boat is shipwrecked. He arrives in a strange country called Lilliput. He meets very small people there. Later he travels to other countries and meets very big people and horses. They all ask Gulliver about his country and how it is different. Are people better or worse there? Gulliver returns home, but his adventures change his ideas and his life.

Chapter 1—I came to Lilliput
I woke up after nine hours. It was daylight and I was on my back. I tried to stand up, but I could not move! I turned my head a little and looked around me. I saw thousands of strings across my body.

… Then something moved on my foot. It moved over my body and up to my face. I looked down and saw a man. He was smaller than my hand. Forty more little men followed him … The man began to speak. His words were strange to me, but I watched his hands. "We will not hurt you," I understood. "But do not try and run away, or we will kill you." I put up my hand and showed him: "I will stay here." Then I had an idea. I also put my hand to my mouth: "I am hungry." The man understood me. He shouted to the people on the ground. A hundred men climbed onto my body and walked up to my mouth. They carried food for me. It came from the king, they told me later.

Reading

1 Look at the picture of Gulliver from the book *Gulliver's Travels*. Answer the questions.
1. Where is he?
2. What is happening?
3. How do you think the little people feel?

2 Read the Introduction and the extract from Chapter 1. Were your predictions correct?

3 Read the Introduction again. Choose the correct options.
1. Gulliver goes to Lilliput *on vacation* / *by accident*.
2. He meets *very big* / *very small* people there.
3. He meets horses *in the same place* / *in another country*.
4. After his adventures, Gulliver *changes* / *doesn't change* his life.

Gulliver's boat is shipwrecked.

4 Read the extract from Chapter 1. Answer the questions.
1. What happened when Gulliver woke up?
   He couldn't move because he was tied up.
2. How are the Lilliputians different from Gulliver?
3. How many men were on Gulliver?
4. How does Gulliver talk to the little man?
5. How do the people help him?
6. What type of ruler does Lilliput have?

My Literature File

5 Take notes about a book you have read. It can be about a journey or an experience of a strange new place. Think about:
- when and where the story happens
- who is/are the main character(s)
- new places he/she goes (they go) to
- new people he/she meets (they meet)
- what happens in the end

6 Write an Introduction to the book. Add photos or pictures. Use your notes from Exercise 5 to help you.

6 That's Life!

Grammar
Have to, don't have to, must, mustn't; Predictions with will, won't, might

Vocabulary
- Household chores;
- Feelings adjectives

Speaking
Giving advice (should, shouldn't)

Writing
A problem page

Word list page 77
Workbook page 109

Vocabulary • Household chores

1 Match the pictures (1–16) to these phrases. Then listen, check and repeat.
2.27

clear the table	cook a meal	do the dishes	do the ironing
do the laundry	feed the cat	hang out the laundry	load the dishwasher
make your bed 1	mow the lawn	set the table	sweep the floor
take out the trash	vacuum the floor	walk the dog	wash the car

2 Complete the sentences with the household chores from Exercise 1.

1 First, *cook a meal* and *set the table*. Then you can eat.
2 …. with all the dirty plates or, if you don't have a dishwasher, …. after the meal.
3 If there are pieces of food under the table, …. or …. .
4 When you have dirty clothes, …. , and then …. to dry.
5 If your clothes are wrinkled, …. .
6 When the trash can in the kitchen is full, …. .
7 …. every day. Pets can't live without food.
8 When the grass is too high, …. .
9 …. every day. Dogs need a lot of exercise.
10 …. on the driveway so it looks nice and clean.

3 In pairs, ask and answer.

1 What chores do you do at mealtimes?
   I always set and clear the table, and I sometimes cook dinner on Saturdays.
2 What chores do other people in your family do?
3 What other chores do you do in the house?

Brain Trainer Unit 6
Activity 2
Go to page 115

Reading

1 Read the webpage quickly. Choose the best title.
1 The World's Laziest Teenager
2 Teens Work Harder Than Their Parents
3 Today's Teens Don't Do Chores

2 Read the webpage again. Are these statements true (T) or false (F)?
1 Cleaning the bathroom is a more popular chore with teenagers than doing the ironing. *F*
2 More than half of all teenagers have never cooked a meal.
3 Dr. Sheila Green thinks teenagers are lazy.
4 She thinks teenagers will be good at their jobs.
5 Dan Sparks thinks that many teenagers do a lot of homework.
6 He thinks it's more important that teenagers do homework, sports and music than chores.
7 Linda Fiorelli makes her children do chores.
8 Linda Fiorelli thinks children don't learn anything when they do chores.

3 What about you? In pairs, ask and answer.
1 How much free time do you have every day?
2 How much time do you spend on household chores?
3 Do you think you do a fair share of the household chores? Why?/Why not?

> How much free time do you have every day?

> Not much—I do a lot of sports after school.

> I have a lot of free time—about two or three hours, I think.

TeenWorld.com

A study of American teenagers has found that most of them have never done any household chores. Many young people aged 11 to 16 don't have to make their bed. Thirty-five percent have never cooked a meal, sixty-three percent have never done the ironing, and more than seventy-five percent have never done the laundry or cleaned the bathroom.

Dr. Sheila Green is one of the authors of the study. "This information is very worrying," she says. "Every year, teenagers are getting lazier. Real jobs in the real world will be very difficult for them."

Dan Sparks, from the parents' website FamilyFirst.com, disagrees. "Young people today work very hard—harder than their parents, sometimes. Many of them have to do three hours of homework every night. Playing on a sports team or learning a musical instrument can take a lot of time too, and these activities are an important part of teenagers' lives. If we want young people with good test scores and also some interests outside school, we shouldn't give them chores."

Linda Fiorelli, author of *The Happy Home*, feels very differently. "It's about respect, not time. Even my five-year-old son has to set the table every day. It takes one minute, but it's important. Children share the house with their parents, so they must share the jobs around the house, too. That's fair, and it teaches good habits for the future."

Grammar • Have to/Don't have to

Affirmative
I/You/We/They have to set the table.
He/She/It has to set the table.

Negative
I/You/We/They don't have to set the table.
He/She/It doesn't have to set the table.

Questions
Do you have to do any chores?
Yes, I do./No, I don't.
Does he have to do any chores?
Yes, he does./No, he doesn't.

Grammar reference Workbook page 96

1 Study the grammar table. Choose the correct options to complete the rules.

1 We use *have to* when something is / isn't necessary.
2 We use *don't have to* when something is / isn't necessary.

2 Find more examples in the article on page 65.

3 Make sentences and questions.

1 clear / the table / has / She / to
   She has to clear the table.
2 the dog / don't / to / We / have / walk
3 I / Do / do / have / any chores / to / ?
4 doesn't / vacuum / the floor / He / to / have
5 They / the laundry / to / hang out / have
6 go / Why / you / have / to / do / ?

4 Complete the sentences. Use the verbs and the form of *have to*.

1 We *have to clean up* (clean up) our bedroom every week.
2 My parents …. (not cook) dinner tonight. We're going to a restaurant.
3 He …. (help) me! I can't do it on my own.
4 I'm really dirty! I …. (take) a shower before I go out.
5 …. (they/do) any homework tonight?
6 My sister …. (not make) her bed in the morning because she's only three.

5 Make questions with *have to*.

1 Clara and David / cook dinner?
   Do Clara and David have to cook dinner?
2 Mom / clean the living room?
3 Dad / feed the cat?
4 Clara and David / load the dishwasher?
5 Clara / wash the car?
6 David / clean up his bedroom?

6 Look at the note. Answer the questions in Exercise 5.

1 *No, they don't. Dad has to cook dinner.*

Chores for today

cook dinner	Dad
clean the living room	Mom
feed the cat	David
load the dishwasher	Clara and David
wash the car	Dad
clean up his bedroom	David

• Must/Mustn't

Obligation
I must leave now. It's late.
I have to help my mom.

No obligation
I don't have to cook any meals.

Prohibition
You mustn't talk in the library.

Grammar reference Workbook page 96

7 Study the grammar table. Do these words mean the same thing?

1 *must* and *have to*
2 *mustn't* and *don't have to*

Unit 6 • That's Life!

8 Replace the words in bold in each sentence so they have the same meaning. Use these words.

> I don't have to   I have to   ~~I must~~   I mustn't

1 **I have to** take out the trash. *I must take out the trash.*
2 **It isn't necessary to** mow the lawn.
3 **I must** do a lot of chores.
4 **I can't** swim here.

9 Choose the correct options.

I'm on a swimming team, and it's hard work. We ¹ *must / don't have to* swim for an hour before school. I ² *mustn't / have to* get up at 6 a.m. because school starts at 8:30, and we ³ *mustn't / don't have to* be late for class! We ⁴ *mustn't / have to* practice every morning from Monday to Friday. On Saturdays there are swim meets, and we ⁵ *must / don't have to* be fast if we want to stay on the team. On Sundays there are no meets, so we ⁶ *mustn't / don't have to* go to the swimming pool. I love Sundays!

10 Make true sentences about your country. Use the correct form of *must, mustn't, have to* or *don't have to*.

1 When you're a baby, you …. go to school.
2 Students …. be polite to their teachers.
3 You …. use your cell phone in class.
4 We …. wear a school uniform.
5 You …. throw trash in the street.

Pronunciation /ʌ/ and /yu/

11a Listen and repeat. Think about the pronunciation of the underlined *u*.

> b<u>u</u>s   conf<u>u</u>sed   m<u>u</u>seum
> <u>u</u>nder   <u>u</u>pset   <u>u</u>sually

b Listen and repeat. Then practice saying the sentences.

1 We don't use gloves in summer.
2 Some of us saw a funny sculpture at the museum.
3 Tuesday was a beautiful, sunny summer's day.
4 My mom made some tuna for lunch.

Vocabulary • Feelings adjectives

1 Look at these words. Check the meaning in a dictionary. Listen and repeat.

> confident   confused   disappointed
> embarrassed   fed up   glad   grateful
> guilty   jealous   lonely   nervous
> relaxed   relieved   upset

Word list page 77
Workbook page 109

2 Match the sentences to the words from Exercise 1.

1 I was really worried, but now everything's OK. *relieved*
2 It's not fair! Why can't I have that?
3 I was hoping for a better result.
4 Thank you so much!
5 My exam starts in a minute. Help me!
6 My exam starts in a minute. I think I can do well on it.
7 No one ever talks to me.
8 I'm so sorry that I hurt your feelings.

3 Read the short texts. How do the people feel? Make sentences using these words.

> confused   embarrassed   ~~fed up~~
> glad   guilty   jealous
> ~~nervous~~   relaxed   upset

1 It's Sam's first day at a new school. He's been to three different schools in the last three years.
Sam is nervous, and he's fed up because he has to change schools so often.
2 Ginny thinks she sees her friend in the street. She runs up to him and says hello. But this person is Connor, and he's never met Ginny before.
3 Jack loves Emily, and Emily loves Jack, but Sophie loves Jack, too. She cries when she sees him. Jack wants Sophie to be happy.
4 Ben doesn't have to do anything today, so he's lying in the sun. It's a beautiful day.

Brain Trainer Unit 6 Activity 3
Go to page 115

Chatroom Giving advice

Speaking and Listening

1 Look at the photo. Answer the questions.
   1 Who has a problem?
   2 What do you think it is?

2 Listen and read the conversation.
2.32 Check your answers.

3 Listen and read again. Choose the correct options.
2.32
   1 Ruby *is / isn't* happy.
   2 She *has / hasn't* finished her homework.
   3 She usually does her homework *on the weekend / on school nights*.
   4 She *has to / doesn't have to* do chores on school nights.
   5 *Ruby / Ruby's parents* usually walk(s) the dog.
   6 Ruby *goes / doesn't go* to climbing club.

4 Act out the conversation in groups of three.

Tom What's wrong, Ruby? You look kind of fed up.
Ruby I am. I've done six hours of homework today!
Tom Maybe you should take a rest.
Ruby A rest? I wish! I haven't even started my math, and that'll be really hard …
Ella You won't have any problems with it, I'm sure. You're great at math! But maybe you shouldn't do all your homework on the weekend, Ruby.
Ruby I don't have enough time for homework on school nights.
Ella Why don't you talk to your parents about your chores? Maybe *they* can walk the dog in the evening, and you can study.
Ruby No, they're too busy. I might stop going to climbing club so I have more time.
Tom I don't think you should stop climbing, Ruby. You love it!

Say it in your language …
What's wrong?
I wish!

Unit 6 • That's Life!

5 Look back at the conversation. Complete these sentences.

1 Maybe you *should* take a rest.
2 Maybe you .... do all your homework on the weekend.
3 Why .... you talk to your parents?
4 I don't .... you should stop climbing.

6 Read the phrases for giving advice.

Positive	Negative
Maybe you should …	Maybe you shouldn't …
I think you should …	I don't think you should …
Why don't you …?	

7 Listen to the conversation. What two pieces of advice does Tom give Ella? Act out the conversation in pairs.
2.33

Ella I can't ¹ find my school sweater!
Tom Why don't you ² clean up your room?
Ella No, I can't do that. ³ I don't have time now. I know! I can ⁴ wear your sweater.
Tom I don't think you should do that. ⁵ It's too big. Maybe you should ⁶ borrow a sweater from Ruby.

8 Work in pairs. Replace the words in purple in Exercise 7. Use these words and/or your own ideas. Act out the conversations.

> I can't find my cell phone!

> Why don't you look in the living room?

1 do my homework / find a birthday present for Mom / sleep at night

2 ask your sister for help / buy that bag / read a book in bed

3 She never helps. / I can't afford it. / I hate reading.

4 skip school / give her a pen / buy a new bed

5 You're too lazy. / It's too boring. / It's too expensive.

6 work harder / look for something at the market / drink hot chocolate before bed

Grammar • Predictions with *will, won't, might*

Definite

I think she'll be relieved.
You won't have any problem, I'm sure.
Will they finish it?

Possible

I might see them tomorrow. I'm not sure.
He might not like the movie.

Watch Out!
will not = won't
might not = ~~mightn't~~

Grammar reference Workbook page 96

1 Study the grammar table. Complete the rules with *will* or *might*.

1 We use .... when we are sure about something in the future.
2 We use .... when we aren't sure about something in the future.
3 The contracted form of .... is *'ll*.
4 The contracted form of .... is *won't*.

2 Choose the correct options in Ruby's predictions.

1 Ella and Tom *will / might* go to the movies with me. They haven't decided.
2 Ash *won't / might not* like the movie. He hates romantic comedies.
3 Bad weather *won't / might not* be a problem at an indoor swimming pool.
4 I'm sure the math test *will / might* be difficult.
5 I *won't / might not* pass the test. I'm not sure.

3 Complete the predictions. Use *will* or *might* and contracted forms where possible.

1 One day I*'ll be* (be) famous. I know it!
2 My team .... (win) the game. We're pretty good, but the other team is pretty good, too.
3 I .... (not finish) my English homework tonight. I'm not sure.
4 They think he .... (arrive) after lunch.
5 .... (you/have) time to wash the car?

Unit 6 • That's Life!

Reading

1 Look at the picture of a teenager of the future. How is his life different from the lives of teenagers today?

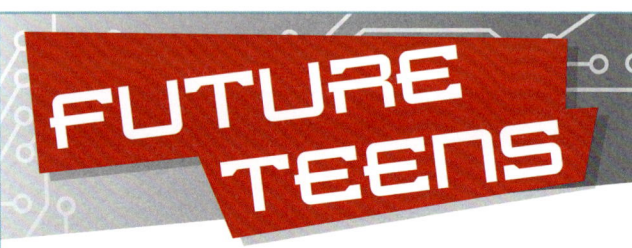

FUTURE TEENS

What kind of life will teenagers have fifty years from now? No one can be sure, but experts have made some interesting predictions.

1 The home
Robots will make the beds, sweep the floor and do the laundry, so teenagers won't have to do many chores. Parents and teenagers might have a more relaxed relationship because of this. Or will they just find other things to argue about?

2 School
Some people might travel to school, but most people will study on their home computers and have virtual classes with the world's best teachers. One teacher might have a million students! All the classes will be in English, and everyone around the world will take the same exams.

3 Free time
Teenagers won't go to cafés and movie theaters with friends, but they won't be lonely. They'll have fun in a virtual world and go to amazing virtual parties with their favorite stars.

4 Entertainment
The movies of today will seem very boring because you can't change the story as you watch. In fifty years, all entertainment will be interactive—there will be no difference between video games and movies.

5 Fashion
Teenagers will be fatter than today because they won't do much exercise, so the most popular clothes will be very big and baggy. Global warming will bring changes in fashion, too. There will be air conditioning inside a lot of clothes—a big help in the hot temperatures around the world.

In fifty years, you will be old and gray. What will you think of the teens of the future?

Key Words

relationship	argue
virtual	baggy
global warming	air conditioning

2 Read the magazine article and check your answer to Exercise 1.

3 Read these headings. Which paragraph do you think will mention these things? Read the article quickly to check.

clothes 5	chores	exams	languages
parents	parties	video games	

4 Read the article again. Answer the questions.
1. Why might parents and their teenage children have a better relationship in the future?
   Because robots will do the teenagers' chores.
2. How will classes in the future be different from classes today? Find three differences.
3. Will teenagers enjoy their free time?
4. What will their parties be like?
5. What will future teenagers think of our movies?
6. Why will there be changes in fashion?

5 Which predictions in the article do you think are
1 correct?   2 silly?   3 exciting?   4 scary?

> "There will be no difference between video games and movies." I think that's correct because it's starting to happen now.

Listening

1 Listen to some teenagers of the future. Match the conversations (1–4) to the topics (A–D).

A home
B school
C free time
D fashion

Listening Bank Unit 6 page 119

Unit 6 • That's Life!

Writing • A problem page

1 Read the Writing File.

> **Writing File** Linking words: reason and result
>
> - You can introduce a reason with *because*.
>   I feel guilty **because** I broke my dad's cell phone.
> - You can introduce a result with *so*.
>   I broke my dad's cell phone, **so** he's really angry with me.

2 Read the problem page from a magazine. Find the linking words of reason and result.

Problem Page

My mom works in a restaurant on Saturday nights, so I have to babysit my six-year-old sister. All my friends have fun together then, but I can't be with them. It isn't fair! What should I do?

Lateesha

I'm sure your mom is very grateful for your help on Saturdays, but you should talk to her about your problem. Choose a time when she isn't busy because it'll be easier to think of an answer to the problem then.
For example, someone else might be happy to babysit your sister some weeks. Other weeks, invite some friends to your house. You'll have more fun at home with your friends there. Cook them some nice food and watch a movie together. But remember, you mustn't make a lot of noise because your sister has to sleep. And clean up the house when they've left so your mom doesn't have to do any chores after a long evening at work.
You and your mom might have a lot of other good ideas, too. Good luck!

3 Complete the sentences with *because* or *so*.

1. I'm tired *because* I went to bed late last night.
2. He's jealous of his sister .... she's better at sports than him.
3. You've finished your homework, ... now you can watch a DVD.
4. I didn't do well in the race, ... I'm a little sad.
5. She's really upset .... her best friend yelled at her.

4 Read the problem page again. Answer the questions.

1. Who should Lateesha talk to about her problem? When?
   She should talk to her mom when she isn't busy.
2. What idea does the writer have so that Lateesha can go out with her friends?
3. What idea does the writer have so that Lateesha can have more fun at home?
4. What two pieces of advice does the writer give about the second idea?

5 Read about James's problem. Answer the questions. Take notes.

> I moved to a new town last year. I have a lot of friends around the world because I play online games in my free time, but everyone at school is really unfriendly. I'm starting to feel pretty lonely. How can I make new friends here?
>
> *James*

1. Is it normal to feel lonely in James's situation?
2. Should he talk to anyone about his problem?
3. Are school friends more important than online friends? Why?/Why not?
4. What can he do to make friends at school?
5. How do you think he'll feel after a few months?

6 Write a letter giving advice to James. Use "My letter" and your notes from Exercise 5.

> **My letter**
>
> **Paragraph 1**
> General advice for this problem
> **Paragraph 2**
> Specific ideas that might help
> **Paragraph 3**
> Encouraging ending

> **Remember!**
> - Use linking words for reason and result.
> - Use the vocabulary in this unit.
> - Check your grammar, spelling and punctuation.

Refresh Your Memory!

Grammar • Review

1 Make sentences and questions with *have to*.

1 we / learn English at school
   We have to learn English at school.
2 you / study French?
3 my sister / not / do any homework
4 she / practice the piano every day
5 she / do any chores?
6 I / get up early for school
7 my parents / not / start work early

2 Complete the text with these words.

| don't | ~~have~~ | has | must | mustn't | to |

My brother and I ¹ *have* to stay with my grandparents this week. It's fun, but they have a lot of rules. For example, we ² .... use our cell phones in the house because they hate cell phones. I ³ .... call my friends on the home phone. My brother ⁴ .... to walk the dog every day, but I ⁵ .... have to do that because I have a bad leg. I have ⁶ .... help Grandma with the cooking and ironing instead.

3 Complete the conversation. Use *will*, *won't* or *might* and the verbs.

A Do you want to come to the Smugglers concert on Saturday? I'm sure you ¹ *will enjoy* (enjoy) it.
B I ² .... (not be) here on Saturday, so I can't come with you.
A Where ³ .... (you/be)?
B In the mountains with my cousins.
A The weather forecast says it ⁴ .... (snow) in the mountains on the weekend. They're not sure.
B Cool! We ⁵ .... (go) snowboarding then, or we ⁶ .... (not do) anything. It's horrible outside when it's too cold and windy.

Vocabulary • Review

4 Match the beginnings (1–6) to the endings (a–f) of the sentences.

1 You should walk   a the cat.
2 She never does   b the dog.
3 Can you please mow   c the ironing.
4 Remember to feed   d the lawn?
5 I don't have to wash   e the trash.
6 We have to take out   f the car.

5 Complete the sentences with the correct feelings adjectives.

1 I like Mr. Green. I'm *glad* he's our teacher.
2 I'm really n _ _ _ _ _ _ about the concert. I might forget the words to all the songs!
3 I think someone stole my purse! Oh no, it's here. I'm so r _ _ _ _ _ _ _ !
4 You've really helped me. I'm so g _ _ _ _ _ _ _ .
5 I said some terrible things to her. I feel really g _ _ _ _ _ about that now.
6 I'm sure I can do it. I'm feeling very c _ _ _ _ _ _ _ _ .

Speaking • Review

6 Complete the advice for these situations. Then listen and check.
2.36

1 **A** I'm late for school again!
  B Why *don't you* get up earlier?
2 **A** I want to go to Antarctica on vacation.
  B I .... you should do that. You hate cold weather!
3 **A** When I sweep the floor, it takes hours!
  B Maybe .... vacuum the floor instead.
4 **A** I'm feeling pretty relaxed about the exams.
  B I .... should be more worried. The exams are very important!
5 **A** When I load the dishwasher, I usually break a plate.
  B Maybe .... do your chores so quickly.

Dictation

7 Listen and write in your notebook.
2.37

✓ My assessment profile: Workbook page 132

Unit 6 • That's Life!

Real World Profiles

Ben Powell's Profile

Age
19 years old

Home country
US

My favorite things ...
theater, music, helping to prevent bullying

Reading

1 Read Ben's profile and look at the photos. Correct the mistakes in this sentence. Then read the article quickly to check.

Ben lives in Canada and has performed in a movie for people with bullying problems.

2 Read the article. Answer the questions.
2.38

1 What does Ben like to do?
He likes to play music and act.
2 Who worked with Ben on the play?
3 What did audience members see in the play?
4 What are some of the consequences of bullying?
5 What was the message of the play?

Ben's Story

Ben has enjoyed performing since he was three years old. Now nineteen, he is a musician (he plays the guitar and the trombone), a singer and an actor.

Ben and other students in his high school worked on a project with a very special message. Together with their drama teacher, they developed a play to present the consequences of bullying. They called it *Teen Reality*. Ben and his classmates helped with different parts of the dramatic production. They wrote the script, designed the set and acted in the play.

What was *Teen Reality* like? The audience walked through scenes showing a teen who is bullied, teenagers who bully others and those who witnessed the situation. The different scenes also presented the consequences of bullying, such as mental health issues and substance abuse. The students' production was a success. It became popular in their community, and it even appeared on a local television station.

Ben graduated from high school and started college, where he studies multimedia communications. He plans to join more organizations that work to prevent bullying. "My goal is to show people that there is no good excuse for bullying, no matter what the reason is," he says.

Key Words

| play | consequences | bullying |
| script | set | |

Class discussion

1 Are there problems with bullying in your country?
2 Are there any programs to help prevent bullying?
3 What can teenagers do to help prevent bullying?

Unit 6 • That's Life! 73

Review 2

Grammar • Present perfect

1 Complete the sentences with the Present perfect form of the verbs.

1 *Have* you *ever been* (be) to Russia?
2 No. But I …. (always want) to go there.
3 I …. (never try) Japanese food.
4 Kelly …. (not finish) her project.
5 My brother …. (always want) to be a pilot.
6 The students …. (not do) their homework again.
7 Where …. you …. (be)? I …. (not see) you for a long time.

• Present perfect vs Past simple

2 Complete the conversations with the Present perfect or Past simple form of the verbs.

A [1] *Have* you *ever ridden* (ride) a camel?
B Yes, I [2] …. (ride) one. I [3] …. (take) a trip through the desert in Morocco once.
A When [4] …. you …. (go) to Morocco?
B We [5] …. (spend) a week there last year.
A When [6] …. you …. (come) back from vacation?
B I [7] …. (fly) back last night.
A What [8] …. (be) it like?
B Great! [9] …. you …. (ever go) to Florida?
A No, I [10] …. (not).

• Present perfect + *for* and *since*; How long?

3 Make sentences with *How long?* Complete the answers with *for* or *since*.

1 **A** you / live / in this house?
   How long have you lived in this house?
2 **B** …. I was a child—so, …. fifteen years!
3 **A** your father / work / in the bank?
4 **B** …. five years.
5 **A** you have / the same hairstyle?
6 **B** …. I was about six!
7 **A** you know / your best friend?
8 **B** …. three years.
9 **A** your class / study / English?
10 **B** …. we were in elementary school.

• Past simple with *just*

4 Complete the sentences with *just* and the Past simple.

1 **A** Something smells delicious in your kitchen. *Did you just bake* a cake? (bake)
2 **B** Yes! I …. it out of the oven. (take)
3 I'm really tired. I …. for a run around the park. (go)
4 Stella …. back from vacation. (arrive)
5 I …. my math homework—after two hours! (finish)
6 I'm crying, because I …. a sad movie on TV. (watch)

• Have to/Don't have to

5 Rewrite the sentences using the correct form of *have to* or *don't have to*.

1 It's essential to wear a helmet on a bike.
   You have to wear a helmet.
2 It's not essential to book tickets in advance.
   You …. tickets in advance.
3 Swimmers need swimming caps. It's a rule.
   Swimmers …. wear swimming caps.
4 You can sit down if you are tired.
   You …. stand.
5 You aren't allowed to arrive late.
   You …. on time.
6 You can have lunch at school or at home. It's your choice.
   You …. have lunch at school.

• Must/Mustn't

6 Make rules with *must* or *mustn't* for these signs.

1 NO PARKING HERE
You mustn't park here.

2 KEEP OFF THE GRASS

3 DON'T EAT OR DRINK IN THE THEATER

4 BE CAREFUL

5 NO SMOKING

6 NO RIGHT TURN

- **Predictions with *will, won't, might***

7 Choose the correct option.
1. Look at those dark storm clouds. It *won't / will* rain later.
2. I'm not sure if I'm going to Mark's party. I *will / might* go.
3. They've been together for a really long time. I'm sure they *might / will* get married.
4. This answer *might / will* be right. I'm not sure.
5. I promise—I *might not / won't* tell anyone your secret.

Speaking • Doubt and disbelief

1 Complete the conversation with these words.

| believe | impossible | ~~kidding~~ | Really |

A Have you heard about this amazing coincidence? A man was walking under a window at the top of a building when a baby fell.
B You're ¹ *kidding*!
A No, it's true. And he was passing at just the right time, so he caught the baby in his arms!
B No! ² .... ?
A Yes, I read it in the paper. And then the same thing happened a few years later.
B I don't ³ .... it.
A It happened to the same man, outside the same building!
B That's ⁴ .... !
A I know, it's the strangest thing.

- **Asking for information**

2 Put the conversation in the correct order.
- *1*. Excuse me, can you help me? I'm looking for the museum. Do you know where it is?
- .... It's a nice walk from here, or you can take a bus.
- .... Yes, I do. It's just across the river, on the left.
- .... Oh yes, there are a lot of restaurants there.
- .... I'd like to walk. But is it far?
- .... OK, so we have to cross the river. How can we get to the river?
- .... That doesn't sound too far. And are there any good places to eat near there?
- .... No, it's about a twenty-minute walk.

- **Giving advice**

3 Complete the conversation with these phrases.

| I don't think you should worry | Maybe you should tell |
| ~~Why don't you talk~~ | You shouldn't pretend |

A What's wrong? You look really upset.
B I feel awful about my science exam results. I don't know how I'm going to tell my parents I did so badly. But I'm really bad at science, and I want to study drama instead.
A ¹ *Why don't you talk* to your parents about it?
B The trouble is, they think I really like science.
A ² .... them the truth.
B They'll be upset. After all, they're both doctors.
A ³ .... about that. They'll understand. ⁴ .... you're interested in something when you aren't.
B Yes, maybe you're right.

Vocabulary • News and media

1 Match the phrases (1–8) to their definitions (a–h).
1. an online diary *h*
2. the title of a newspaper article
3. a formal question-and-answer session with a person
4. a sudden news announcement
5. a person who writes newspaper articles
6. a newspaper article
7. a person who gives the news on TV
8. a news show that can be downloaded on an MP3 player

a interview
b journalist
c headline
d news flash
e news anchor
f podcast
g report
h blog

Review 2   75

Review 2

- **Adverbs of manner**

2 Complete the sentences with these adverbs.

angrily	carefully	early	fast
late	loudly	~~quietly~~	sadly

1 Please enter the room *quietly*—students are taking exams.
2 Can you speak more …. ? I can't hear you—it's very noisy in here.
3 Please drive ….—the roads are dangerous.
4 He's a fantastic athlete. He can run so …. .
5 "Go away," he said, quietly but …. .
6 I thought it would be a funny movie, but it ended so …. I cried.
7 If you don't get up soon, you'll arrive at school …. for your classes.
8 It's best to arrive ….—then we'll get the best seats in the theater.

- **Vacation**

3 Match the verbs (1–8) to the words (a–h) to make vacation phrases.

1 book   a a travel blog
2 eat   b camping
3 go   c in a hotel
4 pack   d a flight
5 stay   e a tent
6 get   f a tan
7 put up   g your bag
8 write   h out

- **Meanings of *get***

4 Replace *get* using a different verb with the same meaning.

1 When my parents get old, I'll take care of them.
   When my parents become old, I'll take care of them.
2 Can you get some milk when you go to the store?
3 What time will we get home?
4 Did you get an email from Laura about her party?
5 Get off the bus when you see a big gray building in front of you.
6 The dog ran very fast to get the ball.

- **Household chores**

5 Match the verbs (1–8) to the words (a–h) to make household chores.

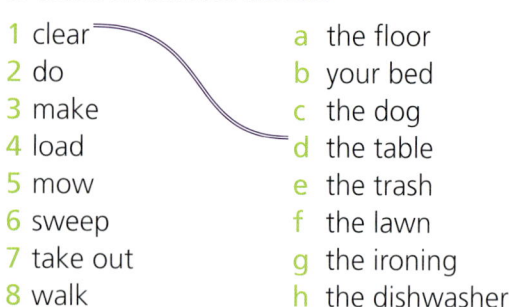

1 clear   a the floor
2 do   b your bed
3 make   c the dog
4 load   d the table
5 mow   e the trash
6 sweep   f the lawn
7 take out   g the ironing
8 walk   h the dishwasher

- **Feelings adjectives**

6 Complete the sentences with these adjectives.

confident	confused	disappointed	glad
grateful	~~jealous~~	nervous	upset

1 Don't be *jealous* of people who seem to have more than you do.
2 My exam is tomorrow, but I'm not …. . I worked hard, so I'm …. I'll do well.
3 Could you explain that to me again? I'm …. .
4 Thank you very much. I'm very …. for your help.
5 Carla's …. because her cat died.
6 I'm so …. you're back! I missed you.
7 I'm …. that I didn't get the job.

76 Review 2

Word list

Unit 4 • In the News

News and media

blog	/blɑg/
current affairs show	/ˈkʌrənt əˈfɛrz ʃoʊ/
headline	/ˈhɛdlaɪn/
international news	/ˌɪntɚˈnæʃənəl ˈnuz/
interview (n, v)	/ˈɪntɚˌvyu/
journalist	/ˈdʒɝnl-ɪst/
local news	/ˌloʊkəl ˈnuz/
national news	/ˌnæʃɔnl ˈnuz/
news anchor	/ˈnuz ˌæŋkɚ/
news flash	/ˈnuz flæʃ/
newspaper	/ˈnuzˌpeɪpɚ/
news website	/ˈnuz ˌwɛbsaɪt/
podcast	/ˈpɑdkæst/
report (n, v)	/rɪˈpɔrt/

Adverbs of manner

angrily	/ˈæŋgrəli/
badly	/ˈbædli/
carefully	/ˈkɛrfəli/
carelessly	/ˈkɛrlɪsli/
early	/ˈɝli/
fast	/fæst/
happily	/ˈhæpəli/
hard	/hɑrd/
late	/leɪt/
loudly	/ˈlaʊdli/
patiently	/ˈpeɪʃəntli/
quietly	/ˈkwaɪətli/
sadly	/ˈsædli/
slowly	/ˈsloʊli/
well	/wɛl/

Unit 5 • Enjoy Your Vacation!

Vacation

book a flight	/ˌbʊk ə ˈflaɪt/
book a hotel	/ˌbʊk ə hoʊˈtɛl/
buy souvenirs	/ˌbaɪ ˌsuvəˈnɪr, ˈsuvəˌnɪr/
check into a hotel	/ˌtʃɛk ˌɪntʊ ə hoʊˈtɛl/
eat out	/ˌit ˈaʊt/
get a tan	/ˌgɛt ə ˈtæn/
get lost	/ˌgɛt ˈlɔst/
go camping	/ˌgoʊ ˈkæmpɪŋ/
go sightseeing	/ˌgoʊ ˈsaɪtˌsiɪŋ/
lose your luggage	/ˌluz yɚ ˈlʌgɪdʒ/
pack your bag	/ˌpæk yɚ ˈbæg/
put up a tent	/ˌpʊt ʌp ə ˈtɛnt/
stay in a hotel	/ˌsteɪ ɪn ə hoʊˈtɛl/
take a trip	/ˌteɪk ə ˈtrɪp/
write a travel blog	/ˌraɪt ə ˈtrævəl blɑg/

Meanings of *get*

arrive	/əˈraɪv/
become	/bɪˈkʌm/
bring	/brɪŋ/
buy	/baɪ/
move	/muːv/
receive	/rɪˈsiːv/
walk	/wɔːk/

Unit 6 • That's Life!

Household chores

clear the table	/ˌklɪr ðə ˈteɪbəl/
cook a meal	/ˌkʊk ə ˈmil/
do the dishes	/ˌdu ðə ˈdɪʃɪz/
do the ironing	/ˌdu ði ˈaɪɚnɪŋ/
do the laundry	/ˌdu ðə ˈlɔndri/
feed the cat	/ˌfid ðə ˈkæt/
hang out the laundry	/ˌhæŋ aʊt ðə ˈlɔndri/
load the dishwasher	/ˌloʊd ðə ˈdɪʃˌwɑʃɚ/
make your bed	/ˌmeɪk yɚ ˈbɛd/
mow the lawn	/ˌmoʊ ðə ˈlɔn/
set the table	/ˌsɛt ðə ˈteɪbəl/
sweep the floor	/ˌswip ðə ˈflɔr/
take out the trash	/ˌteɪk aʊt ðə ˈtræʃ/
vacuum the floor	/ˌvækyum ðə ˈflɔr/
walk the dog	/ˌwɔk ðə ˈdɔg/
wash the car	/ˌwɑʃ ðə ˈkɑr/

Feelings adjectives

confident	/ˈkɑnfədənt/
confused	/kənˈfyuzd/
disappointed	/ˌdɪsəˈpɔɪntɪd/
embarrassed	/ɪmˈbærəst/
fed up	/ˌfɛd ˈʌp/
glad	/glæd/
grateful	/ˈgreɪtfəl/
guilty	/ˈgɪlti/
jealous	/ˈdʒɛləs/
lonely	/ˈloʊnli/
nervous	/ˈnɚvəs/
relaxed	/rɪˈlækst/
relieved	/rɪˈlivd/
upset	/ʌpˈsɛt/

7 Make a Difference

Grammar
Be going to and *will*;
First conditional

Vocabulary
Protest and support;
Verb + preposition

■ **Speaking**
■ Persuading

■ **Writing**
A formal letter

Word list page 111
Workbook page 110

Vocabulary • Protest and support

1 Match the items in the photos (1–12) to these words. Then listen, check and repeat.
3.1

banner
charity
collection
demonstration
donation
fundraising event
march   1
petition
sign
sit-in
slogan
volunteer

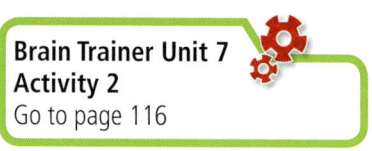

2 Complete the sentences with the words in Exercise 1.
1 Students are having a *sit-in* at school today.
2 This T-shirt has an interesting …. on it.
3 Did you sign the …. against the new road?
4 A …. or sign always carries a strong message.
5 We're taking up a …. for a local charity.
6 They're hosting a dinner as a …. . They want to make a lot of money for the hospital.
7 There are a lot of …. for the fun run. We have a lot of help.

3 **What about you?** In pairs, ask and answer.
1 Have you ever made a donation to a charity? Which one?
2 Have you ever been a volunteer? Who for?
3 Do you have a T-shirt with a slogan on it? What does the slogan say?
4 Have there been any marches or sit-ins in your city or town? What were they for?

> Have you ever made a donation to a charity?

> Yes, I have. I've made donations to the World Wildlife Fund.

**Brain Trainer Unit 7
Activity 2**
Go to page 116

78   Unit 7 • Make a Difference

Reading

1 Look at the text and the photos. Answer the questions.
1. What type of text is it? An article, a letter, a pamphlet?
2. What do you think the topic is?

2 Read and check your answers to Exercise 1.

3 Read the text again. Match the headings to paragraphs A–D.
1. Why did this happen? *B*
2. What are Elephant Family's plans?
3. What's the problem?
4. How can you help?

4 Read the text again. Answer the questions.
1. Where do Asian elephants live?
   In India, Thailand, Malaysia and Indonesia.
2. How many Asian elephants are there?
3. How do the elephants look for food?
4. Why do people kill the elephants?
5. What are "elephant corridors"?
6. What type of event is Elephant Parade?
7. How can you help the charity Elephant Family?

5 In pairs, ask and answer.
1. Do you think Elephant Parade is a good idea? Why?/Why not?
2. Have there been any outdoor art exhibitions in your city or town? Describe them.

Dana Point Elephant Parade

You don't usually see elephants in southern California, but you'll probably meet one near the beach this weekend! This summer there are going to be dozens of elephant sculptures around beaches, parks and resorts in Dana Point, California. They're part of an art exhibition called Elephant Parade. Elephant Parade works with the charity Elephant Family. With your help, we're going to save the Asian elephant.

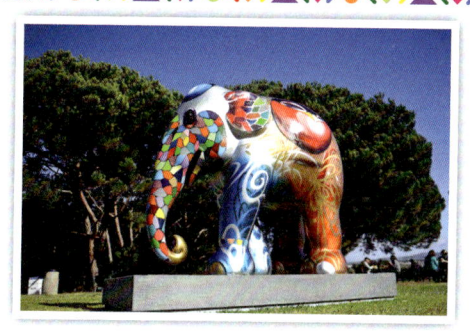

A ....
Today there are only 25,000 Asian elephants in India, Thailand, Malaysia and Indonesia. A hundred years ago there were 200,000 elephants in these countries.

B ....
The elephants are competing with people for food and space. Asian elephants travel from forest to forest, looking for food. Today the forests are getting smaller, and the elephants go through villages to get to them. People in the villages protect their land and kill the elephants. In thirty years there won't be any elephants unless we do something.

C ....
The charity Elephant Family is going to make "elephant corridors." They're special roads between the forests where elephants can travel safely. There's already one in India, but we need many more.

D ....
Come and see Elephant Parade. The parade isn't a march, so we won't have banners or slogans. It's a fundraising event. After the exhibition we're going to sell the sculptures. You can buy smaller elephants or T-shirts at our website, or make a donation and sign our petition.

The future is in our hands. Help us save the Asian elephant.

Grammar • Be going to

Affirmative
There are going to be dozens of elephant sculptures.
The charity is going to make "elephant corridors."

Negative
There aren't going to be dozens of elephant sculptures.
The charity isn't going to make "elephant corridors."

Questions and short answers
Are they going to make them?
Yes, they are./No, they aren't.
What are they going to do?

Grammar reference Workbook page 98

1 Study the grammar table. Choose the correct option to complete the rule.

1 We use **be going to** to talk about *the future* / *the present*.
2 **Be going to** introduces *a prediction* / *a plan*.

2 Make conversations. Use *going to/not going to*.

1 **A** What / you / do on the weekend?
  B I / buy a new T-shirt.
  What are you going to do on the weekend?
  I'm going to buy a new T-shirt.
2 **A** It's jeans day tomorrow. What / you / wear?
  B Well, I / not wear my school uniform!
3 **A** They / take up / a collection for charity.
  B I / not make / a donation. I don't have any money.
4 **A** You / sign the petition against the new supermarket?
  B Yes, I am. I don't agree with it.
5 **A** My brother / be a volunteer at the school marathon.
  B What he / do?
6 **A** You / take a banner to the march?
  B Yes, I am. I / write a slogan on it, too.

Pronunciation Going to

3a Listen to these sentences. Do you hear *gonna* or *going to*?

1 I'm going to play football.
2 We're going to a concert.
3 What time is it going to start?
4 Are you going to the party?

b Listen again and repeat.

4 Complete the conversation. Then listen and check.

A Hey, Connor. ¹ *Are you gonna play* (you/play) football in the park on Saturday?
B No, I'm not. I ² …. (make) a banner.
A What for?
B Sunday is Earth Day. There ³ …. (be) a march.
A Earth Day? ⁴ …. a lot of people …. (go)?
B Yes, they are. And after the march, we ⁵ …. (have) a concert in the park.
A That's cool. Who ⁶ …. (play)?
B Taylor Swift and Lorde.
A Wow! What time ⁷ …. (start)?
B At three o'clock. ⁸ …. (you/come)?
A Yes, I am!

5 Imagine you are organizing a concert for a charity. In pairs, ask and answer.

1 Which charity / help?
2 Which group / play?
3 the concert / be at school?
4 What time / begin and end?
5 How / make money? you / sell T-shirts, CDs?

> Which charity are you going to help?

> We're going to help the World Wildlife Fund.

Unit 7 • Make a Difference

• *Will* or *be going to*

Predictions

In 30 years there won't be any Asian elephants.
You'll probably meet one near the beach this weekend.

Plans or intentions

We're going to save the Asian elephant.

Grammar reference Workbook page 98

6 Look at the sentences. Are they plans or predictions?

1 Your horoscope says, "The color red will bring you good luck." *prediction*
2 I'm not going to go to school tomorrow— it's Saturday!
3 We're going to go to the basketball game this weekend. We've bought our tickets.
4 I don't think he'll pass his exams. He never does his homework.
5 My friend has problems with math, so I'm going to help him after school.
6 I'm sure we'll have fun at the party. Everyone will be there.

7 Complete the sentences. Use *will* and *going to*.

1 I / do my homework now. Maybe I / call my friends later.
I'm going to do my homework now.
Maybe I'll call my friends later.
2 We / play baseball on Saturday. We hope we / win.
3 He / get a bike for his birthday. Maybe it / be red.
4 Lola is sick. She / not go school today. Perhaps she / feel better tomorrow.
5 We / watch a DVD tonight. I hope it / be a scary movie.
6 I / not go to the charity event. Maybe people / not notice.

Vocabulary • Verb + preposition

1 Look at the phrases. Check the meaning of each in a dictionary. Listen and repeat.
3.5

agree with	apologize for	argue with
believe in	care about	decide on
disapprove of	hope for	insist on
know about	protest against	worry about

Word list page 111 **Workbook** page 110

2 Match the beginnings (1–6) to the endings (a–f) of the sentences.

1 She apologized *a*
2 We have to decide
3 I don't believe
4 Everyone hopes
5 Do you know
6 On his birthday Aidan insisted

a for her bad behavior.
b in charity. People should help themselves.
c for a better world.
d about the party on Saturday night?
e on getting a pet snake.
f on a topic for our school project.

3 Complete the text. Use the correct prepositions.

Walk around the Barrio Gótico in Barcelona and you'll see strange marks on the street. They say "city residents" on one side and "tourists" on the other. People are worried ¹ *about* the number of tourists in the city, and the marks show people are protesting ² .... this. Many people agree ³ .... the protest. "Sometimes I can't cross the street because there are so many tourists," says Nuria Cugat. "They're noisy and rude. They don't care ⁴ .... our city." Julio Sanchez disapproves ⁵ .... the protest. "I can't argue ⁶ .... Nuria about the noise, but we need tourism."

4 In pairs, ask and answer.

1 How often do you argue with your parents?
2 Do you worry about exams?
3 What things do you care about?
4 Have you ever protested against something?

Brain Trainer Unit 7
Activity 3
Go to page 116

Unit 7 • Make a Difference

Chatroom Persuading

Speaking and Listening

1 Look at the photo. Answer the questions.
1. Where are the teenagers?
2. What do you think they are doing?
3. What do the slogans on their T-shirts say?
4. What do you think Ella is saying to Ruby?

2 Listen and read the conversation. Check your answers.

3 Listen and read again. Answer the questions.
1. Why are they protesting?
   The city council is going to close down the library.
2. What does Ella want Ruby to do?
3. Why can't Ruby join them?
4. What does Ella say they have?
5. What does Ash say Ruby can do?
6. Why does Tom think the demonstration is important?

4 Act out the conversation in groups of four.

Ruby Hi, guys. What are you doing here?
Tom We're protesting.
Ruby What are you protesting against?
Ash The city council is going to close down the library. They say that people don't use it, but that's not true!
Ella Will you sign our petition? If you sign it, you'll help to keep the library open.
Ruby I suppose so.
Tom Hey, why don't you join us?
Ruby Sorry, I can't. I have homework to do.
Ella Come on, Ruby. It'll be fun. Look, we have T-shirts with slogans.
Ash And you can hold my sign. It's better than doing homework.
Ruby I don't know.
Tom But it's important. We all use the library, and we care about what happens to it. If we don't protest, they *will* close it. I'm sure you don't want that to happen.
Ruby OK, I'll do it. You win! Where's my T-shirt?!

Say it in your language …
Come on.
I suppose so.
You win!

5 Look back at the conversation. Who says what?

1 Come on, Ruby. *Ella*
2 It'll be fun.
3 It's better than doing homework.
4 I'm sure you don't want that to happen.

Persuading	Responding
Come on. It'll be fun.	I don't know.
It's better than … + *ing*.	OK, I'll do it.
I'm sure you …	

6 Read the phrases for persuading and responding.

7 Listen to the conversation. What is Ruby persuading Tom to do? In pairs, act out the conversation.
3.7

Tom This is ¹ hard!
Ruby Come on, Tom. It'll be fun.
Tom I don't know. This is the first time I've ² been on a skateboard. I'm going to ³ fall!
Ruby No, you're not. I'm sure you'll be fine.
Tom OK, you win! … Hey, this is easier than I thought.
Ruby Yes, and it's better than ⁴ playing soccer!

8 Work in pairs. Replace the words in purple in Exercise 7. Use these words and/or your own ideas. Act out the conversations.

> This is boring!

> Come on …

1 hard / dangerous / tiring

2 played the guitar / ridden a scooter / trained for a marathon

3 hurt my fingers / fall / stop after 5 km

4 listening to music / playing a computer game / going for a bike ride

Grammar • First conditional

if + Present simple, will + infinitive

If we don't protest, they will close the library.

will ('ll) + infinitive > if + Present simple

They will close the library if we don't protest.

Grammar reference Workbook page 98

1 Study the grammar table. Choose the correct options to complete the rules.

1 We use the First conditional to talk about *possible* / *impossible* situations.
2 The Present simple after *if* refers to events in *the future* / *the present*.

2 Complete the sentences.

1 If I *buy* (buy) a new T-shirt, it *won't have* (not have) a slogan.
2 You …. (not pass) your exam if you …. (not review) your notes.
3 If you …. (care about) your friend, you …. (help) him.
4 He …. (laugh) if you …. (tell) him a joke.
5 If we …. (have) a school sit-in, there …. (be) trouble!
6 She …. (have) fun if she …. (go) to the fundraising event.
7 If they …. (be) worried about the library, they …. (sign) the petition.
8 I …. (get) angry if you …. (argue) with me.

3 Complete the sentences in your own words.

1 If I save some money, … .
2 If I have some time tonight, … .
3 If it's sunny this weekend, … .
4 If I have a birthday party, … .
5 If we go on vacation, … .

4 In pairs, ask and answer about your sentences in Exercise 3.

> What will you do if you save some money?

> I'll buy a new watch.

Unit 7 • Make a Difference

Reading

1 Look at the title of the magazine article and the photos. What do you think the article is going to be about?

Eco World

Do Something Different ...

You don't have to go on a march or sign a petition to make a difference and change things. This week in *Eco World* magazine, we look at other ways you can protest.

350.org

350.org is an organization that protests against climate change. It believes that if you do something different, more people will listen. In 2010 it organized the world's biggest art exhibition, called eARTh. People in sixteen different countries made huge pictures on the ground outside. You could only see the pictures from satellites in space.

In the Delta del Ebro in Spain, an artist named Jorge Rodriguez-Gerada created a picture of a little girl named Galla. Galla was worried about global warming, and the picture is about what might happen to the Ebro River. Hundreds of volunteers helped Jorge make it, and thousands of people have seen it on Google Earth™.

Critical Mass bike rides

On a Friday evening in September 1992, sixty cyclists met in San Francisco and went on a bike ride. There was a lot of traffic on the roads, but there were a lot of bikes too, so cars stopped for them. This was the world's first Critical Mass bike ride. Cyclists on the ride were protesting against cars and pollution. They wanted safer roads for cyclists.

Today over 200 cities have CM bike rides. Rides take place on the last Friday of every month, and there are often more than 1,000 cyclists. The protests have made a difference, and many cities now have bicycle lanes and "car free" days. This year the biggest bike ride will be on Earth Day in Budapest. "There are going to be 80,000 people on 80,000 bikes!" says one cyclist. Imagine that!

Key Words
organization   climate change
traffic   pollution
bicycle lanes

2 Read the article. Copy the table and match the organizations to the things they are protesting against.
3.8

cars	climate change
dangerous roads	environmental damage
global warming	pollution in cities

350.org	CM bike rides
climate change	

3 Read the article again. Answer the questions.
1 How does 350.org believe you can make people listen?
   If you do something different, more people will listen.
2 What was unusual about the art exhibition?
3 What did Jorge Rodriguez-Gerada do?
4 Where was the first CM bike ride?
5 Why did cars stop for the bikes?
6 How have the CM protests made a difference?

4 Think about protests that have happened in your country. Choose one example.
1 What was the problem?
2 How did people protest? What did they do?
3 Did the protest make a difference?

Listening

1 Listen to the radio interview about a charity.
3.9 Answer the questions.
1 Who does Link Romania help?
2 What does it do?

Listening Bank Unit 7 page 120

Writing • A formal letter

1 Read the Writing File.

> **Writing File Letter writing**
>
> When you write a letter or email to a magazine, you can use these phrases.
> - **Opening**
>   *Dear (+ name of person or magazine),*
> - **Say why you are writing**
>   *I am writing to comment on …*
> - **Closing**
>   *Kind regards, (+ your name)*
>   *Best wishes, (+ your name)*

2 Read the letter. Match the parts (1–5) to (a–e).

a reason for writing
b opening the letter *1*
c closing the letter
d What action can we take?
e What is the problem?

Eco World Letters Page

1 Dear Eco World,
2 I am writing to comment on your article about biking to school in this week's magazine. In the article, you say not many kids bike. I think this is because there are not enough bicycle lanes. Kids don't feel safe on a bike, so most of them go to school by car (including me!).
3 If people don't bike, there will be more traffic on the roads, and more pollution. This is bad for the environment.
4 How can we encourage people to get on their bikes? The solution is clear: we need more bicycle lanes. If we sign a petition asking for bicycle lanes, maybe the city council will listen. If there are more lanes, more kids will bike to school!
5 Kind regards,
Samantha Kippel

3 Read the letter again. Answer the questions.

1 Why is Samantha writing to *Eco World*?
   She wants to comment on an article about biking.
2 Why don't kids bike to school?
3 Why is this bad for the environment?
4 What does Samantha suggest?

4 Match these problems (1–4) to the headlines (a–b) from *Eco World*.

1 There won't be a place for kids to play.
2 We won't have a place to study.
3 There won't be a place for people to read.
4 We won't have a place for people to walk.

> **a Park Is Going, Parking Lot Is Coming!**
>
> Our local park is going to become a parking lot. A lot of people use the park—there's a children's play area and a café there.

> **b Library Is Going to Close**
>
> The city council has decided to close our library. They say that the library is too expensive.

5 Choose one article from Exercise 4. Take notes about the problems. Try to think of a solution.

6 Write a letter to *Eco World* about the article you chose in Exercise 5. Use "My formal letter" and your notes from Exercise 5.

> **My formal letter**
>
> **1 Opening**
> *Dear Eco World,*
> **2 Reason for writing and the problem**
> *I am writing to comment on the article about …*
> *In the article, you say that …*
> **3 Action**
> *How can we save our …?*
> **4 Closing**
> *Kind regards,/Best wishes,*

Remember!
- Use phrases from the Writing File.
- Use the vocabulary in this unit.
- Check your grammar, spelling and punctuation.

Refresh Your Memory!

Grammar • Review

1 Complete the sentences. Use *going to* and these verbs.

have	not go	not watch
~~review~~	send	wear

1 I *'m going to review* my notes tonight. I have an exam tomorrow!
2 We …. the concert this weekend. We don't have tickets.
3 …. they …. a picnic? It's a beautiful, sunny day.
4 He …. the football game. He hates football!
5 …. she …. invitations to the party?
6 It's cold outside. …. you …. a coat?

2 Complete the sentences. Use *will* or *going to* and the verbs.

1 Maybe I*'ll wear* (wear) a dress to the party. I don't know.
2 Brett is wearing his bike helmet. He …. (ride) his bike.
3 Let's go on a boat ride. Maybe we …. (see) a dolphin.
4 She …. (go) skiing this winter. She's booked a hotel in the Alps.
5 Maybe it …. (be) sunny later. Then we can go to the beach.
6 I …. (watch) my favorite TV show tonight. It starts at 7.

3 Match the beginnings (1–6) to the endings (a–f) of the sentences.

1 If we sign the petition, *f*
2 If she says "sorry,"
3 If they go shopping,
4 He won't be happy
5 If I tell you the truth,
6 You'll get a sunburn

a will you be friends again?
b if his team loses.
c will you keep it a secret?
d they'll buy some new clothes.
e if you lie in the sun too long.
f we'll make a difference.

Vocabulary • Review

4 Choose the best options.

1 There's a *march* / *sit-in* today. It starts downtown and ends at the park.
2 I gave $5 to UNICEF today. Have you ever made a *donation* / *collection* to a charity?
3 It was a successful *petition* / *fundraising event*. We took in $5,000 for the hospital!
4 I like the *slogan* / *banner* on your T-shirt. "Save the Planet" is cool!
5 The WWF is *a charity* / *a collection* that helps animals.
6 Protestors were carrying *signs* / *slogans* with *signs* / *slogans* on them. They said, "Save Our Jobs!"

5 Complete the sentences with these words.

agree	apologized	argue	care
insists	know	~~protested~~	worried

1 A lot of people *protested* angrily against the new highway.
2 I …. for forgetting my homework.
3 Do you …. about endangered animals?
4 I'm not …. about my exams. I know I'll do OK.
5 Do you …. with me?
6 Do you …. about Zoe's party this weekend?
7 I never …. with my girlfriend.
8 Our teacher always …. on silence in class.

Speaking • Review

6 Put the conversation in the correct order. Then listen and check. *3.10*

Girl I don't want to make these banners. I'm bored. *1*
Boy No, it won't. I'm sure we'll finish them quickly.
Girl OK, you win! It's better than doing it on my own.
Boy Come on, I'll help you. It'll be fun.
Girl I don't know. There's a lot of work to do. It's going to take a long time!

Dictation

7 Listen and write in your notebook. *3.11*

✓ **My assessment profile:** Workbook page 133

Global Citizenship File

FAIRTRADE: CHOCOLATE

Fairtrade

1 What is it?

Shopping connects us with millions of people around the world. These people work on farms and in factories, and they make the things we buy. Many of them come from developing countries, and big companies don't pay them much money.

Fairtrade companies give people a fair price for the work they do. They help people take care of their families and buy the things they need. They also make sure that people work in safe conditions. Sometimes you pay a little more for Fairtrade products, but if we pay a little more, people in other countries will have better lives.

Fairtrade Fact File: Chocolate

2 ....

Chocolate comes from cocoa beans on cocoa trees. Cocoa trees grow in countries with a tropical climate. Cameroon, Ivory Coast and Ghana all grow cocoa beans. Countries like these are often very poor.

3 ....

Cocoa farmers grow the cocoa beans. Many farmers earn less than fifty cents a day. They grow their own food, but it's hard for them to pay for other things, like medicine and clothes.

4 ....

Farmers get more money for their work, so they can buy medicine and send their children to school. Some villages now have access to clean water, too. Farmers also get help and advice about farming. They learn new skills, so they become better farmers.

5 ....

- Find Fairtrade chocolate at your local supermarket, then vote with your wallet and buy it!
- Encourage your friends and family to do the same.
- Make your school Fairtrade-friendly. Design a poster, or start a petition.
- Ask for Fairtrade products (not just chocolate!). There are more than 3,000 Fairtrade products to choose from!

Key Words

farms	factories
developing country	fair price
tropical climate	vote

Reading

1 Read the article quickly. Match the headings (A–E) to the paragraphs (1–5).

A What is it? 1
B Who makes it?
C How does Fairtrade help?
D What can we do?
E Where is it from?

2 Read the article again. Are these statements true (T) or false (F)?
3.12

1 Big companies pay people more money. F
2 Fairtrade products are sometimes more expensive than other products.
3 Countries that grow cocoa beans are usually rich.
4 Cocoa farmers have to pay for their food.
5 Fairtrade helps farmers improve their work.
6 There aren't many Fairtrade products.

My Global Citizenship File

3 Choose another Fairtrade product and take notes about it. Think about:
- where it is from
- who grows or makes it
- how Fairtrade helps
- what we can do to help

4 Write a Fairtrade fact file about your product. Add photos or pictures. Use your notes from Exercise 3 to help you.

Unit 7 • Make a Difference

8 Danger and Risk

Grammar
Second conditional;
Relative pronouns

Vocabulary
Extreme adjectives;
Illness and injury

Speaking
Talking about health

Writing
An application form

Word list page 111
Workbook page 111

Vocabulary • Extreme adjectives

1 Listen and repeat. Then match the normal adjectives (1–10) to the extreme
3.13 adjectives in the box. Check your answers in a dictionary.

| awful |
| burning |
| ~~excellent~~ |
| exhausted |
| freezing |
| furious |
| huge |
| terrifying |
| thrilled |
| tiny |

1 good *excellent*
2 small
3 hot
4 cold
5 scary
6 big
7 bad
8 pleased
9 angry
10 tired

2 Match the comments (1–3) to the photos (a–c).

1 It's huge and he's tiny. It looks freezing cold.
2 It's an excellent picture. It looks terrifying.
3 It's an awful place. I think she's exhausted.

3 Complete the conversations with extreme adjectives.
3.14 Listen and check, then practice with a partner.

A Was the movie really good?
B It was ¹ *excellent*.

A Are you very tired?
B Yes, it's late. I'm ² ..... .

A Brr! It's really cold in here.
B You're right. It's ³ ..... . Do you have a sweater?

A Is he really pleased with his grade on the exam?
B He's ⁴ ..... . He did really well.

A Was your mom really angry that you stayed out late?
B Yes, she was. She was ⁵ ..... !

4 What about you? In pairs, ask and answer.

Have you ever …
• watched a terrifying movie?
• gotten an excellent grade on an exam?
• picked up a huge spider?

**Brain Trainer Unit 8
Activity 2**
Go to page 116

Reading

1 You are going to read about an unusual job. Before you read, look at the photo and answer the questions.

1 What type of job do you think it is?
2 How do you think the person feels?
3 Why do you think she does it?

2 Read the interview quickly and check your answers.

3 Work in pairs. Find these numbers in the interview. What do they refer to?
- 80
- 1,000,000
- 8
- 100

4 Read the interview again. Are these statements true (T) or false (F)?

1 In today's movies, computers create most of the stunts. F
2 Stunts can be very expensive.
3 Naomi doesn't earn much money.
4 She was tired after her first job.
5 She has had a lot of accidents.
6 She thinks a police officer's job is more dangerous.

5 In pairs, ask and answer.

1 Do you think Naomi's job is dangerous?
2 Can you think of other dangerous jobs?
3 Do you know anyone who does a dangerous job?
4 Would you like to be a stuntman or woman? Why?/Why not?

Interview: Naomi Daniels

Interview

Naomi Daniels

Today's action movies are often thrilling adventures with amazing stunts. Computers create some of these stunts, but stuntmen and stuntwomen do most of them. In some action movies, there are more than eighty stuntmen and women, and one stunt can cost over a million dollars! It's an exciting job, but what about the risks? We interviewed stuntwoman Naomi Daniels.

Naomi, why are you a stuntwoman?
Because it's an excellent job! I earn a lot of money, I travel around the world, I meet famous people, and I never do the same thing twice. If I weren't a stuntwoman, I'd do extreme sports. But stunts are more fun!

Can you remember your first job?
Yes, I can. It was a car race in the desert. It was burning hot, and it took eight hours to film. At the end of the day, I was exhausted.

Do you ever worry about the risks?
Sometimes, but I practice a lot, and I'm very careful. I don't usually have accidents, but last year I hurt my leg. I was furious because it was an easy stunt—a jump from a hundred-meter-high bridge!

If I were you, I'd be really frightened!
Well, if I were scared, I wouldn't be a stuntwoman.

Would you be happier if you had an ordinary job?
No, I wouldn't. If I had an ordinary job, I'd be bored. And I don't think my job is dangerous. When I see police officers or firefighters, then I think, "Wow, that's dangerous."

Grammar • Second conditional

| *if* + Past simple, *would* (*'d*) + verb |
| *would* (*'d*) + verb > *if* + Past simple |
| **Affirmative** |
| If I had an ordinary job, I'd be bored. |
| **Negative** |
| If I weren't a stuntwoman, I'd do extreme sports. |
| If I were scared, I wouldn't be a stuntwoman. |
| **Questions and short answers** |
| Would you be happier if you had an ordinary job? |
| Yes, I would./No, I wouldn't. |

Watch Out!
If I were you, I'd be terrified.
= If I ~~was~~ you, I'd be terrified.

Grammar reference Workbook page 100

1 Study the grammar table. Choose the correct options to complete the rules.

1 We use the Second conditional to talk about *probable / improbable* situations or *real / unreal* events.
2 The Past simple after *if* refers to events now or *in the future / in the past*.

2 Choose the correct options.

1 If I could choose any job, I *would be / will be* a firefighter.
2 If I *forgot / forget* my friend's birthday, I would feel embarrassed.
3 He would be furious if you *copied / copy* his homework.
4 If we learned another language, we *studied / would study* Chinese.
5 I would wear a big coat if it *is / were* freezing outside.
6 If she went to bed late, she *is feeling / would feel* exhausted.
7 It *will be / would be* awful if they had an accident.
8 If I could meet anyone in the world, it *would be / will be* Justin Bieber.

3 Complete the text with the correct form of the verbs.

If you ¹ *had* (have) tickets for a huge, terrifying roller coaster ride, what ² .... (you/do)? "I'd go on it," says Joel Alvaro. "If I ³ .... (can) ride roller coasters all day, I ⁴ .... (do) it," he adds, "but I have to go to work." Joel is a teacher—he also loves amusement parks. "If I ⁵ .... (live) in Orlando, Florida, I ⁶ .... (be) thrilled," he says. Orlando has the most roller coaster rides in the world! If he ⁷ .... (be) in Orlando, he ⁸ .... (visit) Disney World every day. But he doesn't. His girlfriend thinks he's crazy. "Roller coasters are fun, but if I ⁹ .... (go) on them all the time, I ¹⁰ .... (get) bored and feel sick!" she says.

4 Look at these situations. Make questions.

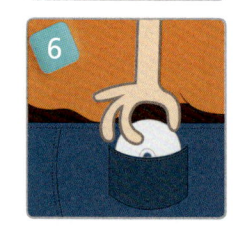

1 you / see / a movie star
What would you do if you saw a movie star?
2 you / find / 50 dollars in the street
3 you / lose / your backpack
4 your friend / break / your cell phone
5 your parents / be / furious with you
6 your friend / steal / from a store

5 In pairs, ask and answer the questions in Exercise 4.

What would you do if you saw a movie star?

I'd ask him or her for an autograph.

Unit 8 • Danger and Risk

Vocabulary • Illness and injury

1 Match the pictures (1–12) to these words and phrases. Then listen, check and repeat.
3.16

a backache	a burn	a cold
a cough	a cut	a fever
a headache	a rash 1	a sore throat
a sprained ankle	a stomachache	a toothache

Word list page 111
Workbook page 111

2 What's wrong with these people?
1 My head hurts. I'm going to take an aspirin.
   a headache
2 I fell down the stairs, and now I can't walk.
3 I can't eat anything. There's something wrong with my tooth.
4 I can't stand straight or lift heavy things.
5 My head feels hot, but I feel cold. I need a blanket.
6 I ate too much. I feel sick.
7 I had an accident. I hurt my finger with a knife.

3 Complete the sentences with the words in Exercise 1.
1 He spilled boiling water on his hand, and now he has a really bad *burn*.
2 My nose is red, and I don't feel very well. I think I have a…. .
3 My…. is so bad it wakes me up at night.
4 I have a….. It hurts when I eat or drink.
5 This…. is awful. I can't stop scratching!

Pronunciation *gh*

4a Listen and repeat. How do we pronounce *gh* in these words?
3.17

| brought | cough | eight | enough |
| high | laugh | rough | thought |

b Copy the table and put the words in Exercise 4a in the correct column. Then listen and check.
3.18

/f/	silent
cough	brought

c Listen and repeat. Pay close attention to the *gh* sound.
3.19
1 It's eight o'clock.
2 Have you had enough to drink?
3 I brought some medicine for your cough.
4 Don't laugh. I thought you were sick!

**Brain Trainer Unit 8
Activity 3**
Go to page 117

Unit 8 • Danger and Risk 91

Chatroom Talking about health

Speaking and Listening

1 Look at the photo. Answer the questions.
1. Where are Tom and Ruby?
2. What's wrong with Ruby?
3. What did Tom do?

2 Listen and read the conversation. Check your answers.
3.20

3 Listen and read again. Answer the questions.
3.20
1. How did Ruby hurt herself?
   She tripped over a cat.
2. Where was the woman?
3. What does Tom do at the O_2 arena?
4. How did Tom hurt himself?
5. What does he think is wrong?
6. Why does Ruby feel sorry for Tom?

4 Act out the conversation in pairs.

Tom	Hi, Ruby. What's the matter?
Ruby	Oh, I hurt my arm.
Tom	How did you do that?
Ruby	Well, I tripped over a cat which ran out from under a car.
Tom	That's awful!
Ruby	The cat was OK, but my arm wasn't. The woman who was in the car brought me here. Oww!
Tom	Are you all right?
Ruby	Don't worry, I'm fine. So why are *you* here?
Tom	I had a silly accident at the O_2 arena.
Ruby	The what?
Tom	The O_2 arena, you know … it's the place where I play soccer.
Ruby	So what happened?
Tom	I was trying to score a goal when I fell over the ball.
Ruby	That's funny, except your leg looks terrible. How does it feel?
Tom	Not too good. I think I have a sprained ankle. And we lost the game!
Ruby	Poor thing!

Say it in your language …
That's awful!
Poor thing!

Unit 8 • Danger and Risk

5 Look back at the conversation. Complete the sentences.

1 *What's* the matter?
2 I … my arm.
3 Are you … ?
4 I'm … .
5 … does it feel?

6 Read the phrases for asking and talking about health.

Asking about health	Responding
What's the matter?	I have a headache/ a sprained ankle/ a toothache, etc.
Are you all right?	I'm fine, thanks.
How does it feel?	Not too good./Pretty bad.
How do you feel?	A little better, thanks.

7 Listen to the conversations. What's wrong with Tom and Ella? Act out the conversations in pairs.
3.21

Ash Hi, Tom. You look awful! What's the matter?
Tom Achoo! I have ¹ a cold.
Ash Poor thing! How do you feel?
Tom Not too good.
Ella I feel awful. I have ¹ a headache.
Ash Can I get you anything?
Ella No, I'm fine, thanks. … OK, maybe ² a hot drink.
Ash You should ³ get some rest, too.

8 Work in pairs. Replace the words in purple in Exercise 7. Use these words and phrases and/or your own ideas. Act out the conversations.

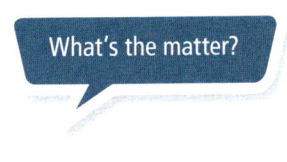

> What's the matter?

> I have a cough.

1 a backache / a sprained ankle / a toothache

2 a hot water bottle / some ice / some medicine

3 go to the doctor / take an aspirin / go to the dentist

Grammar • Relative pronouns

It's the place **where** I play soccer.
She's the woman **who** was in the car.
That's the cat **which** was under a car.

Grammar reference Workbook page 100

1 Study the grammar table. Complete the rule with *who, which* or *where*.

We use relative pronouns to talk about places (…), people (…) and things (…).

2 Choose the correct options.

1 I don't like stories *who* / *which* make me cry.
2 That's the store *which* / *where* I got my shoes.
3 This is the bag *which* / *who* is very heavy. The others are OK.
4 There's the beach *where* / *which* we went swimming last year.
5 She's the girl *who* / *which* is good at soccer.
6 That's the TV show *which* / *who* is all about doctors.

3 Complete the sentences with *who, which* or *where*.

1 I hate movies *which* are scary.
2 He's someone … is very kind.
3 It's the place … we went for Tom's birthday.
4 Those are the jeans … were very expensive.
5 That's the pizza place … I usually go.
6 She's the teacher … is always late.

4 Complete the conversation with *who, which* or *where*.

A There's the boy ¹ *who* won the competition.
B Oh, really? Where was that?
A It was at the skatepark ² … is near the beach.
B I don't know it.
A Well, it's the place ³ … I go on weekends.
B Is it good?
A Yes. It has a café ⁴ … you can meet friends. Look! He's walking this way.
B Is he the tall one?
A No. He's wearing a black T-shirt ⁵ … has a cool slogan.
B Ah yes! There's a girl ⁶ … is talking to him. She's holding a cell phone ⁷ … has a pink cover.
A That's right. Hmm … is she his girlfriend?

Unit 8 • Danger and Risk

Reading

1 Look at the photo. Answer the questions.
1. What's happening in the photo?
2. How does the girl feel? How would you feel?
3. Why do you think people take risks?

This Week's Big Question

Why Are People Risk-Takers?

Recently amazing teenagers have been in the news. Laura Dekker has sailed around the world, Parker Liautaud has skied to the North Pole, and Amelia Hempleman-Adams has skied to the South Pole. These teenagers are all natural risk-takers, but why do they do it? We looked at some popular explanations.

1 It's all about adrenalin

Some scientists believe that risk-takers' bodies don't react to danger like most people's bodies. When we are in danger, our bodies make a chemical called adrenalin. It stimulates our brain and makes us ready to fight or run away. Risk-takers' bodies don't make adrenalin easily, so they take more risks to feel "alive."

2 Little old women don't go snowboarding

Studies have shown that tall people take more risks than small people, women are more careful than men, and older people take fewer risks than younger people. Tall people are often confident, and confident people are not easily scared. Scientists also think that men are more natural risk-takers than women, and that age and experience make people more cautious … or really boring!

3 Be careful what you watch

Recent research asked these questions, too. If you played a computer game about risk-taking, would that make you take risks in real life? And if your parents or friends took risks, would you take them, too? It seems the answer to both questions is yes!

And finally … some researchers say that risk-takers are frequently bored—they often change jobs, and they don't have long relationships. But some people say they are happier. What do you think?

Key Words

risk-taker scientist react
stimulate research

2 Read the magazine article and check your answers to Exercise 1.

3 Find these words in the article. In pairs, try to explain what they mean. Look them up in a dictionary to check.
1. chemical (line 16)
2. confident (line 31)
3. cautious (line 37)
4. frequently (line 50)

4 Read the article again. Answer the questions.
1. What do the teenagers in the introduction have in common? *They are all risk-takers.*
2. Why do risk-takers take risks?
3. Why do tall people take more risks?
4. What happens when we get older?
5. How do risk-takers often feel?

5 In groups, discuss these questions.
1. Are you tall, young and healthy?
2. Do you ever feel scared?
3. Do you love computer games?
4. Are you a risk-taker? Why?/Why not?

Listening

1 Listen to two people talking about a TV show. Answer the questions.
1. What's the show called?
2. Name two things the teenagers have to do.
3. What's the prize?

Listening Bank Unit 8 page 120

Unit 8 • Danger and Risk

Writing • An application form

1 Read the Writing File.

> **Writing File** Completing an application form
> - Read the questions: do you have to write information or choose an answer?
> - If you have to write information, what kind of information is it? (name, date, number?)
> - If you have to choose an answer, read all the answers first
> - Complete the form.
> - Check what you have written.

2 Read the application form for the *Survivor* TV show. Complete the questions with these words.

> how (x2)   how many   what
> where   why

Survivor
Application Form

Send your application form to:
Survivor
51 W 52nd St
New York, NY 10019

Name *Casey MacDonald*   Age *14*

1 .... adventurous are you? (5 = very, 1 = not at all)
   1 ☐   2 ☐   3 ☐   4 ✓   5 ☐

2 .... of the activities have you done? (mark the boxes)
   camping ✓   climbing ✓   sailing ☐   fishing ✓
   cooking ☐

3 If you could visit *one* of these places, ... would you go? Mark the box. Say why.
   the jungle ☐   a desert island ☐   Disney World ✓
   I'd like to go to Disney World because I love roller coasters, and it would be really exciting.

4 .... would your best friend describe you? Circle four words.
   (adventurous)   nervous   (funny)   serious
   (happy)   moody   (friendly)   shy

5 .... are you scared of?
   I'm terrified of losing.

6 .... do you want to be on *Survivor*?
   Because I love trying new things. I also want to be on TV!

3 Match the question words (1–6) to the answers (a–f). What type of information do the answers give (e.g., a number, a date, a place, a person, a reason, a thing)?

1 What *f*
2 Who
3 How many
4 Where
5 When
6 Why

a Because it's my birthday.
b On Friday, June 12.
c My friends.
d At the pizza place.
e Twelve.
f A party.

4 Read the application form again. Answer the questions.

1 Which activities has Casey never tried?
   sailing and cooking
2 Where would he like to go?
3 Is he a confident person?
4 What is he worried about?
5 Why does he want to be on the show?

5 Copy and complete the application form for you.

> **Remember!**
> - First, read the questions: do you have to circle or mark an answer, or write information?
> - If you have to write information, what kind of information is it?
> - If you have to choose an answer, read all the answers first.
> - Complete the form.
> - Check what you have written in the form carefully.
> - Use the vocabulary in this unit.
> - Check your grammar, spelling and punctuation.

Refresh Your Memory!

Grammar • Review

1 Complete the sentences. Use the Second conditional.

1 If she *didn't have* (not have) homework, she'd watch the action movie.
2 …. (he/travel) abroad if he had more time?
3 They…. (climb) the mountain if it stopped snowing.
4 If you…. (be) famous, would you be my friend?
5 What…. (you/do) if you lost your cell phone?
6 If people…. (not take) risks, would they be happier?

2 Read the sentences. Are the explanations (a and b) true (T) or false (F)?

1 If I could sing, I'd be a pop star.
  a I can sing very well. *F*
  b I can't sing at all. *T*
2 If he went on the roller coaster, he'd enjoy it.
  a He probably won't go.
  b He's going to go.
3 If she worked hard, she'd be at the top of her class.
  a She works hard.
  b She doesn't work hard.
4 If they were good at basketball, they'd be on the school team.
  a They are on the school team.
  b They aren't on the school team.
5 I'd be furious if you broke my MP3 player.
  a You probably won't break it.
  b The MP3 player doesn't work.
6 If I could meet anyone in the world, I'd choose Lady Gaga.
  a You'll probably never meet her.
  b You're going to meet her next week.

3 Choose the correct options.

1 A nurse is a person *who / which* takes care of people.
2 The movie theater is a place *which / where* we can watch movies.
3 There's the girl *which / who* was late for class.
4 Swimming is a sport *who / which* is good for you.
5 Isn't that the hotel *which / where* we stayed?
6 This is the café *where / who* I meet my friends.
7 I like this bag—the one *who / which* is $55.

Vocabulary • Review

4 Replace the words in bold with extreme adjectives.

| awful | ~~exhausted~~ | freezing | furious |
| huge | terrifying | thrilled | tiny |

1 I've studied all day. I'm **really tired**! *exhausted*
2 The burger was **very big**, but he ate it all.
3 Dad was **really angry** when I broke his watch.
4 The bird was **very small**. I held it in my hand.
5 My sister Jenny was **very pleased** with her birthday present.
6 I didn't enjoy the party. The music was **very bad**.
7 It's **really cold** outside. It has started to snow.
8 The horror movie was **very scary**.

5 Match the illnesses and injuries to the definitions.

| a cold | ~~a fever~~ | a headache |
| a sore throat | a sprained ankle | a stomachache |

1 This makes you feel hot and cold. *a fever*
2 Your nose is sore.
3 This hurts when you walk.
4 Your stomach hurts.
5 Your throat hurts.
6 Your head and eyes hurt.

Speaking • Review

6 Complete the conversation with these words. Then listen and check.
3.24

| ~~all right~~ | feel | get | have | how | too good |

Girl You look awful! Are you ¹ *all right*?
Boy No, I'm not ². …. I ³. …. a stomachache.
Girl Poor thing! Can I ⁴. …. you anything?
Boy Maybe a glass of water.
Girl Here you go. ⁵. …. do you ⁶. …. now?
Boy A little better, thanks.

Dictation

7 Listen and write in your notebook.
3.25

✓ **My assessment profile:** Workbook page 134

Unit 8 • Danger and Risk

Real World Profiles

Crina "Coco" Popescu's Profile

- **Age**: 18 years old
- **Home country**: Romania
- **My favorite things …**: climbing, biking, running, swimming, travel, my family and friends

Coco Loves Climbing

In 2011 Crina "Coco" Popescu climbed Mount Sidley, the highest mountain in Antarctica. The views from the top of the mountain were amazing, but the most amazing thing was Coco's age: she was only 16. Today Coco is 18, and she is also the youngest woman to climb the seven highest volcanoes in the world.

Coco started climbing when she was six years old. First, she climbed the mountains around her hometown of Rasnov. Then she started to climb bigger, more dangerous mountains. When she was 10, she climbed the huge Dente del Gigante mountain in the Alps. After the climb, she was exhausted, but also excited … about her next challenge!

So how does she do it? Well, she works very hard. Coco trains every day after school. She also goes running, swimming and biking. If she didn't train, she wouldn't be strong enough to go on expeditions. She doesn't have much time to watch movies, shop or go out with her friends.

Coco is an excellent climber, but she doesn't take risks. In 2009 she was halfway up a mountain in the Himalayas when the weather suddenly changed. It was a dangerous situation and a terrifying experience. She gave up the expedition and went home. Coco was disappointed, but she learned from her ordeal. Today, with the help of her family and friends, she's broken six world records. "I can't thank my parents enough for their support," says Coco. "I'm trying hard to make them proud."

Reading

1 Read Coco's profile. Correct the mistakes in this short text.

Coco is a 16-year-old climber from Romania. Besides climbing, Coco loves biking and skateboarding, and she's also a good swimmer. She doesn't like traveling much, but she loves her family and friends.

2 Read the magazine article. Answer the questions.

1 What did Coco do when she was 16?
She climbed the highest mountain in Antarctica.
2 When did she start climbing?
3 How did she feel after climbing the Dente del Gigante?
4 How is her free time different from her friends' free time?
5 Why did she give up on the Himalayan mountain?
6 How many world records has she broken?

Class discussion

1 Are there any young record breakers like Coco in your country?
2 Are there any mountains in your country? If there are, which is the highest?
3 Which is the highest mountain in the world? Which country is it in?

9 Inventions

Grammar
Present simple passive;
Past simple passive

Vocabulary
Machine nouns and verbs;
Word building

■ **Speaking**
Problems with machines

Writing
An opinion essay

Word list page 111
Workbook page 112

Vocabulary • Machine nouns and verbs

1 Match the pictures (1–8) to these verbs. Then match the pictures (9–18) to these nouns. Then listen, check and repeat.
3.27

| Verbs: | attach | build | communicate 1 | invent |
| | plug in | press | produce | turn on/off |

| Nouns: | battery | button | cable | jack | keyboard |
| | outlet | power cord | remote control | tube 10 | wheel |

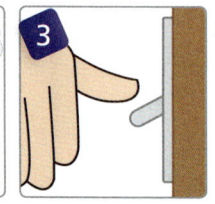

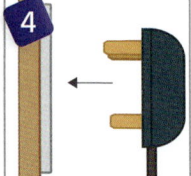

2 Look at the machine and complete the instructions. Use the words in Exercise 1.

MY MARVELOUS ICE CREAM MAKER

¹ *Plug* the power cord into the nearest ² …. .
³ …. the red button to ⁴ …. the machine.
Put eggs, cream and sugar into the different ⁵ …. s.
Use the ⁶ …. on your laptop to write the name of your favorite ice cream.
Turn the ⁷ …. or press the ⁸ …. s on the ⁹ …. .
The machine will ¹⁰ …. some tasty ice cream.
Remember to ¹¹ …. the machine.
Then enjoy!

3 In pairs, take turns describing one of these things. Use words from Exercise 1 and the words below.

| cell phone | flash drive | flashlight |
| tablet | train | TV |

A *It has a battery. Before you can use it, you have to turn it on. You can use it to produce light and to see in the dark.*
B *It's a flashlight!*

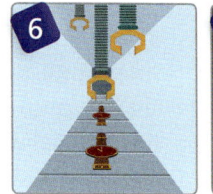

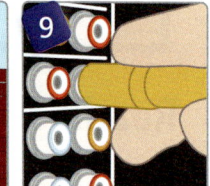

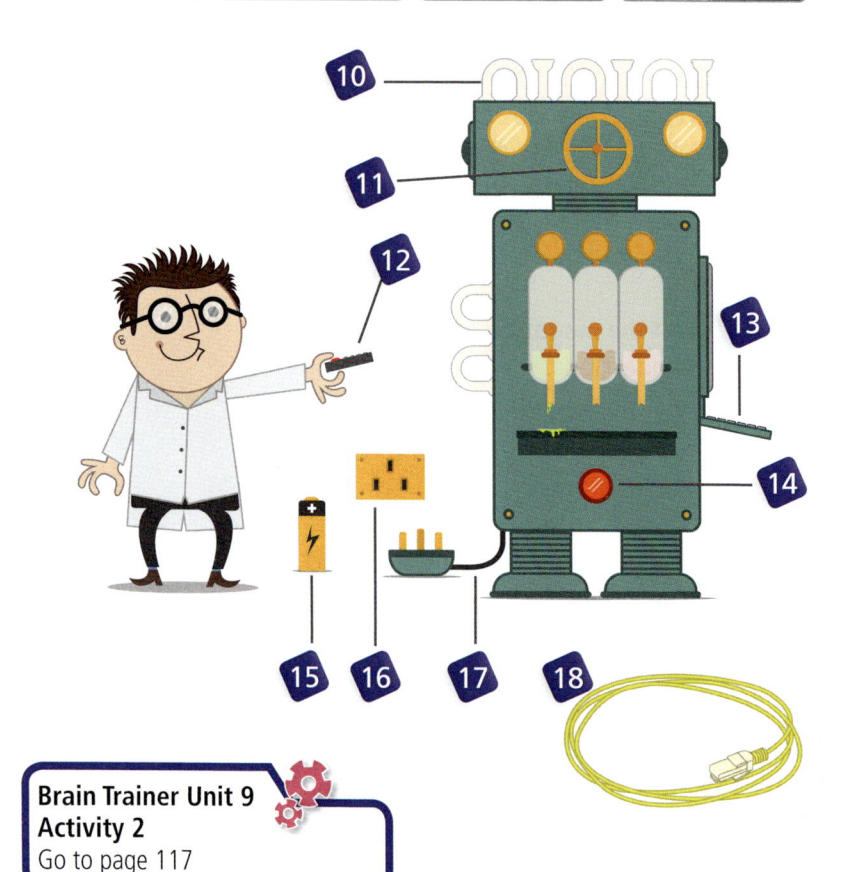

**Brain Trainer Unit 9
Activity 2**
Go to page 117

Reading

1 Think of some famous inventors. What did they invent?

2 Read the magazine article quickly. Match the paragraphs (1–3) to the photos (a–c).

3 Read the article again. Are these statements true (T) or false (F)?
3.28
1. Louis Braille could never see. *F*
2. His system of writing was a completely new idea.
3. Alexander Kendrick's invention can help people with injuries.
4. People should always have a cell phone with them when they are spelunking.
5. Hibiki Kono's invention uses machines that many people have in their homes.
6. He uses his invention to climb the walls in his bedroom.

4 What do you think?
1. Which of the inventions in the photos is
   a the smartest?
   b the most useful?
   c the most fun?
   Say why.

> I think the low-frequency radio is the smartest invention. It's difficult to build a radio, and this radio can do things that other radios can't do.

2. If you were an inventor, what would you invent?

> I would invent a robot that could do all my homework for me!

Teenage Inventors

You don't have to be old with crazy white hair to invent something. Here are some of our favorite young inventors.

1 Louis Braille (1809–1852) was French. He became blind in an accident when he was only three years old. At the age of twelve, he learned about a system of writing with bumps in paper that you feel with your fingers. Louis liked this idea, but the writing was difficult to read. For the next three years, he worked on a similar, but easier system. The result of his work was "Braille" writing. The first book in Braille appeared in 1829, and Braille is still used by blind people today.

2 Sixteen-year-old Alexander Kendrick loves spelunking, but it's a very dangerous activity. When accidents happen underground, it's impossible to communicate with the outside world. Messages that are sent on traditional radios or cell phones can't travel through rock. Alexander has built a special low-frequency radio that works 300 meters underground. It is made with plastic tubes and metal cable, and messages are written on a keyboard. This clever machine might save a lot of lives in the future.

3 Gloves aren't usually used to climb walls, are they? Well, thirteen-year-old Hibiki Kono has invented special gloves! A small vacuum cleaner is attached to each glove. When the vacuum cleaners are turned on, the gloves can carry the weight of a large person on a wall or ceiling. But Hibiki isn't allowed to use the gloves in his bedroom. His mom thinks they're too dangerous.

Grammar • Present simple passive

Affirmative
It is made with plastic tubes.
They are made with plastic.

Negative
The machine isn't made with plastic.
Gloves aren't usually used to climb walls.

Questions and short answers
Is the machine made with plastic?
Yes, it is./No, it isn't.
Are the gloves used to climb walls?
Yes, they are./No, they aren't.

Grammar reference Workbook page 102

1 Study the grammar table. Choose the correct options to complete the rules.

1 We use the passive when we want to focus on *the action / the person or thing doing the action*.
2 We make the Present simple passive with the Present simple of *have / be* and the Past participle.

2 Complete the sentences with the Present simple passive of the verbs.

A lot happens around the world in one minute:
1 A hundred new cars *are produced* (produce).
2 The Internet …. (use) by 64 million people.
3 Twelve million text messages …. (send).
4 10,000 songs …. (download) from the Internet.
5 1.5 million kilograms of trash …. (throw away).

3 Make sentences.

1 our washing machine / run / every day
  Our washing machine is run every day.
2 the cables / not plug in / to the right jacks
3 My laptop isn't working. My homework / not save / on another computer!
4 batteries / not include

4 Make questions. Then ask and answer in pairs.

1 cell phones / allow / in class?
  Are cell phones allowed in class?
2 interactive whiteboards / use / at your school?
3 English / speak / all the time in your English class?
4 your TV / turn on / all evening?

• Active and passive

Active
Blind people use Braille.
You write messages on a keyboard.

Passive
Braille is used by blind people.
Messages are written on a keyboard.

Grammar reference Workbook page 102

5 Study the grammar table. Choose the correct options to complete the rules.

1 With an active verb, the person or thing that does the action goes *before / after* the verb.
2 With a passive verb, we *always / don't always* mention the person or thing that does the action.
3 With a passive verb, we introduce the person or thing that does the action with *by / for*.

6 Change these active sentences into passive sentences. Don't include *by* + noun.

1 People spend seventy-five billion dollars on video games every year.
  Seventy-five billion dollars *are spent on video games every year.*
2 People eat a lot of ice cream in the summer.
  A lot of ice cream …. .
3 They don't sell that candy in my town.
  That candy …. .
4 Teachers give too much homework to students.
  Too much homework …. .

7 Change these active sentences into passive sentences. Include *by* + noun.

1 A hairstylist usually cuts my hair.
  My hair *is usually cut by a hairstylist.*
2 The average teenager sends almost nine hundred text messages every month.
  Almost nine hundred text messages …. .
3 A Japanese company makes those cell phones.
  Those cell phones …. .
4 The sun warms the water in the pool.
  The water in the pool is …. .

Unit 9 • Inventions

Vocabulary • Word building

1 Take the quiz.

2 Listen and check.
3.29

QUIZ

1. **What did Coco Chanel design?**
   a *clothes*
   b planes
   c computers

2. **What is Pablo Picasso's *Guernica*?**
   a a film
   b a book
   c a painting

3. **What was Alexander Graham Bell's most famous invention?**
   a the phone
   b the radio
   c the TV

4. **Who was the author of *Romeo and Juliet*?**
   a Charles Dickens
   b William Shakespeare
   c Agatha Christie

5. **Which company is a famous car producer?**
   a Nokia
   b Ikea
   c Volvo

6. **What is the Taj Mahal?**
   a a mountain
   b a building
   c a river

3 Copy and complete the table.

verb	noun 1: person	noun 2: result
build	builder	¹ *building*
²	designer	design
invent	inventor	³ ....
paint	painter	⁴ ....
produce	⁵	product
write	⁶	writing

Word list page 111
Workbook page 112

4 Complete the text with these words.

> built   designs   inventor
> ~~painted~~   painter   paintings

Leonardo da Vinci ¹ *painted* the *Mona Lisa*, one of the world's most famous ² .... . But he wasn't only a ³ .... . He was also the ⁴ .... of flying machines, musical instruments and hundreds of other things. Some experts have followed his ⁵ .... for a flying machine and have ⁶ .... one that can fly!

Pronunciation /ɪ/ and /i/

5a Listen and repeat.
3.30

> big   build   clean   email
> Internet keyboard   silly   wheel

b Copy the table and put the words in Exercise
3.31 5a in the correct column. Then listen and check.

/ɪ/	/i/
big	clean

c Listen and repeat.
3.32
1. The D on his keyboard disappeared.
2. Build a bigger machine, please.
3. She invented a new, thinner screen.

**Brain Trainer Unit 9
Activity 3**
Go to page 117

Unit 9 • Inventions 101

Chatroom Problems with machines

Speaking and Listening

1 Look at the photo. What do you think the girls are doing?

2 Listen and read the conversation. Check your answer.
3.33

3 Listen and read again. Complete the sentences.
3.33
1 What did Ella make the robot from?
   An aluminum can.
2 What did she find on the Internet?
3 What's the problem with the robot?
4 How does Ella know that the battery is OK?
5 Why didn't she see the red button before?
6 How does the robot break?

4 Act out the conversation in pairs.

Ruby Is that your robot for the science project? It's so cute! Was it made from an aluminum can?
Ella Yes, it was. But it doesn't work.
Ruby What's the problem?
Ella Well, the instructions weren't included in the box. I found some on the Internet, and I've done everything that they say, but the wheels don't move.
Ruby There might be something wrong with the battery. Have you checked it?
Ella Yes. It was only bought yesterday, and it works OK in my flashlight.
Ruby Have you tried pressing that red button?
Ella No, I haven't—it was hidden under the robot's arm. Here goes … Yay! It's working!
Ruby Watch out, Ella! It's going to fall off the table! **CRASH!**
Ella Oh no! It's broken. What am I going to do now?

Say it in your language …
It's so cute!
Here goes.
Yay!

Unit 9 • Inventions

5 Look back at the conversation. Complete the sentences.

1. It doesn't *work*.
2. What's the .... ?
3. Have you .... it?
4. Have you .... pressing that red button?

6 Read the phrases for talking about problems.

Talking about problems with machines	
What's the problem?	It doesn't work. It's broken. The (wheels) don't (move).
Have you tried (pressing that button)?	No, I haven't.
There might be something wrong with the battery. Have you checked it?	

7 Listen to the conversation. What does Ash suggest? Act out the conversation in pairs.
3.34

Ash Let's ¹ watch this DVD on your laptop.
Tom We can't. ² It doesn't work.
Ash What's the problem?
Tom ³ The laptop can't play it.
Ash There might be something wrong with ⁴ the DVD. Have you checked it?
Tom Yes. It works OK ⁵ in the DVD player.
Ash Have you tried ⁶ restarting your laptop?

8 Work in pairs. Replace the words in purple in Exercise 7. Use these words and/or your own ideas. Act out the conversation.

> Let's watch TV.

> We can't. It doesn't work.

1. listen to some music / send Ruby a text
2. my MP3 player / my cell phone
3. there is no sound / it can't send texts
4. the "play" button / the battery
5. and it says "playing" / and I charged it earlier
6. turning it off and on again / standing outside in the yard

Grammar • Past simple passive

Affirmative	Negative
It was made by Ella.	It wasn't made by Ella.
They were bought yesterday.	The instructions weren't included in the box.
Questions	

Was it made from an aluminum can?
Yes, it was./No, it wasn't.
Were the instructions included?
Yes, they were./No, they weren't.

Grammar reference Workbook page 102

1 Study the grammar table. Choose the correct option to complete the rule.

> We form the Past simple passive with the Past simple of *be* / *have* and the past participle.

2 Complete the text with the Past simple passive form of the verbs.

The first cell phones were very big. They ¹ *were used* (use) on trains and planes in the 1920s. A cell phone network ² .... (introduce) in Tokyo in 1979, and other cities soon followed. The first text message ³ .... (send) in Finland in 1993, and later, cell phones ⁴ .... (produce) that could take photos and use the Internet. In 2010 more than five billion cell phones ⁵ .... (own) by people around the world!

3 Change these sentences into the passive. Only include *by* + noun if this is important.

1. People in the US invented the Internet.
   The Internet was invented in the US.
2. Da Vinci didn't build the world's first plane.
3. My friend Jack won the science fair.
4. They didn't tell the students about the exams.
5. My dad designed our house.

4 Make questions in the Past simple passive. Then ask and answer.

1. your favorite photos / take / on a cell phone?
   Were your favorite photos taken on a cell phone?
2. your favorite book / write / a long time ago?
3. your favorite movies / make / in your country?
4. your class / give / a lot of homework last week?

Reading

1 Look at the photos (a–d). Put the inventions in the order that they were invented.

A Book for All Time?

Next time you hold a book in your hands, stop and think. Like most other things in the modern world, it is the result of thousands of years of human invention.

First came the invention of writing, probably about 5,500 years ago. With writing, people did not have to remember everything in their heads. They could communicate with people that they never saw and share their knowledge with future generations.

Later, the Greeks were known throughout the ancient world for their literature, philosophy and science, but their "books" looked very different from the books of today. They were called scrolls. They were difficult to use and took up a lot of space in a library. It was only about 2,000 years ago that books with a lot of pages were invented. With the help of an index at the back, readers could find information more quickly than in a scroll. Before long, scrolls were a thing of the past.

For more than a thousand years, the pages of books were made from animal skin. That changed in the thirteenth century, when Europeans learned about a useful Chinese invention: paper.

But the biggest change for books came around 1439, when Johannes Gutenberg invented the printing press. Before that, books were copied by hand, so they were very expensive. Many more people could afford the books that were produced on a printing press.

These days it is difficult to imagine a world without books. But human invention does not stop. Every year, more stories are bought as e-books and read on a screen.

Will anyone turn the pages of a traditional book in the future, or will books, like scrolls, soon disappear?

Key Words

knowledge   generation   ancient
index   skin   traditional

2 Read the magazine article quickly to check.

3 Read the article again. Are these statements
3.35 true (T) or false (F)?

1 The ancient Greeks invented writing. *F*
2 Greek books had a lot of pages.
3 There were libraries in the ancient world.
4 The first books with pages were made of animal skin.
5 Paper was invented in Europe.
6 Gutenberg's printing press made cheaper books.

4 Read the article again. Answer the questions.
3.35
1 What did people have to do before the invention of writing?
They had to remember everything in their heads.
2 What two problems were there with scrolls?
3 Why were books easier to use than scrolls?
4 What did people use to make books when they stopped using animal skin?
5 For what reasons was the printing press an important invention?
6 Why might books disappear in the future?

Listening

1 What are the advantages and disadvantages of reading on a smart phone?

2 Listen to the conversation. Do they talk about
3.36 any of your ideas in Exercise 1?

Listening Bank Unit 9 page 120

3 In pairs, ask and answer.
1 Do you like these types of stories?
- fantasy   • funny   • historical
- horror   • romantic   • science fiction
2 How many books do you read every year?
3 Do you prefer traditional books or e-books? Why?
4 Will books exist in fifty years? Why?/Why not?

I like funny stories, but I don't like horror or science fiction stories.

Unit 9 • Inventions

Writing • An opinion essay

1 Read the Writing File.

> **Writing File** How to write an opinion essay
>
> In an opinion essay, you need:
> - a title
> - an introduction giving your opinion (*In my opinion, …*)
> - reasons for your opinion, given in a good order (*First, … , Second, … , Finally, …*) with examples (*for example, …*)
> - a conclusion (*In conclusion, …*)

2 Read Alisha's essay. Find words and expressions from the Writing File.

The Most Useful Invention for Teenagers
by Alisha Kent

In my opinion, the most useful invention for teenagers is the smart phone.

First, it's great in an emergency. If someone has an accident or there's a fire, you can call quickly for help. Because of this, parents often feel more relaxed if you have a smart phone with you, and you can stay out longer with your friends.

Second, you can use it to go online when you aren't at home. This is useful in many situations. For example, you can find out the time of the next bus when you're in a café, and look at a map on the Internet when you're lost.

Finally, a smart phone is great entertainment. You can watch movies on it, play games, listen to music and read stories. With a smart phone in your pocket, you never have to be bored, even on a long trip.

In conclusion, the smart phone is a fantastic invention. Teenagers are happier and more independent because of it.

3 Put these parts of an opinion essay in the correct order.

a In conclusion, Edison's inventions were some of the most useful in the world.
b Second, he invented a way to bring electricity to people's homes.
c In my opinion, the world's greatest inventor was Thomas Edison.
d The World's Greatest Inventor   *1*
e First, he invented the lightbulb.
f Finally, he invented a machine that could record and play sound.

4 Read Alisha's essay again. Answer the questions.

1 In Alisha's opinion, what is the most useful invention? *The smart phone.*
2 Why did she choose this invention?
3 In what two situations is it useful?
4 How are teenagers' lives different because of it?

5 You are going to write an essay with this title:

The most important invention of the last 200 years

Choose an invention and take notes about it. Use the questions in Exercise 4 to help you.

- car
- computer
- Internet
- plane
- TV

6 Now write your essay. Use "My essay" and your notes from Exercise 5.

> **My essay**
>
> **Paragraph 1**
> Introduce the invention.
>
> **Paragraphs 2–4**
> Give reasons why it is important—one reason for each paragraph. Include examples of situations that prove your point.
>
> **Paragraph 5**
> Summarize your reasons for choosing this invention.

> **Remember!**
> - Give an introduction with your opinion.
> - Give reasons for your opinion.
> - Write a conclusion.
> - Use words you've practiced in this unit.
> - Check your grammar, spelling and punctuation.

Refresh Your Memory!

Grammar • Review

1 Complete the sentences with the correct passive form (Present simple or Past simple) of the verbs.

1. She *was interviewed* (interview) on the news yesterday.
2. Excuse me! …. (dogs/allow) on the bus?
3. I can't read that. It …. (write) in French.
4. …. (the Internet/use) in the 1950s?
5. That word …. (not spell) correctly. Use a dictionary!
6. Too many trees …. (cut down) every year.
7. The dishes …. (not do) last night.
8. Skateboards …. (invent) in the US in the 1950s.

2 Make sentences and questions in the passive. Only use *by* + noun if necessary.

1. They play football in the park every Saturday.
   Football is played in the park every Saturday.
2. Do people read books at your school?
3. James broke my pen.
4. They don't speak Japanese in Thailand.
5. My grandma made this sweater.
6. We didn't need the tent.
7. Did they make these computers in China?
8. Our friend designed the website.

3 Active or passive? Complete the text with the correct form of the verbs.

In 1901 American inventors Wilbur and Orville Wright [1] *built* (build) a flying machine, but it [2] …. (not design) well enough. It [3] …. (not fly)! "Man will fly, but not in our lifetime," Wilbur [4] …. (say) sadly.
The brothers [5] …. (learn) from their mistakes, however. In 1903 some changes [6] …. (made) to the design, and a new machine [7] …. (build). Wilbur [8] …. (carry) through the air for 59 seconds in the new machine. Some photos [9] …. (take) of this famous moment—the first flight of the world's first plane! Today the names of the Wright brothers [10] …. (know) all around the world, and thousands of people [11] …. (come) to see their plane at the museum in Washington where it [12] …. (keep).

Vocabulary • Review

4 Match the beginnings (1–8) to the endings (a–h) of the sentences.

1 You can write on your computer with a	a tube.
2 Plug the cable into the	b audio jack.
3 The flashlight won't work without a	c remote control.
4 A bicycle has two	d wheels.
5 Please don't press those	e keyboard.
6 You can turn on the TV with a	f outlet.
7 Posters are often sold in a	g battery.
8 Plug the power cord into the	h buttons.

5 Complete the sentences with the correct form of the words.

1. Claude Monet was a famous French *painter* (paint).
2. What …. (produce) is Apple™ famous for?
3. Her …. (write) is difficult to read.
4. I love his …. (design) for the new school building.
5. The …. (build) has to put a new roof on the house.
6. Everyone thinks it's a useful …. (invent).

Speaking • Review

6 Complete the conversation with the correct form of these words. Then listen and check.
3.37

> check   go   ~~not work~~   problem   try   wrong

Dad It's time to practice your electric guitar!
Boy I can't. It [1] *isn't working*.
Dad What's the [2] …. ?
Boy It can only play really quietly. Listen!
Dad There might be something [3] …. with the cord. Have you [4] …. it?
Boy But it's new. It was bought yesterday.
Dad Er … Have you [5] …. plugging it in?
Boy Yikes! I forgot! Here [6] …. . Yay! It's working!

Dictation

7 Listen and write in your notebook.
3.38

✓ **My assessment profile:** Workbook page 135

Unit 9 • Inventions

Science File

Did you know that 0.039% of the gas in the Earth's atmosphere is carbon dioxide (CO_2)? CO_2 is a greenhouse gas: it absorbs infrared radiation. Because of this, too much CO_2 in the atmosphere causes global warming.

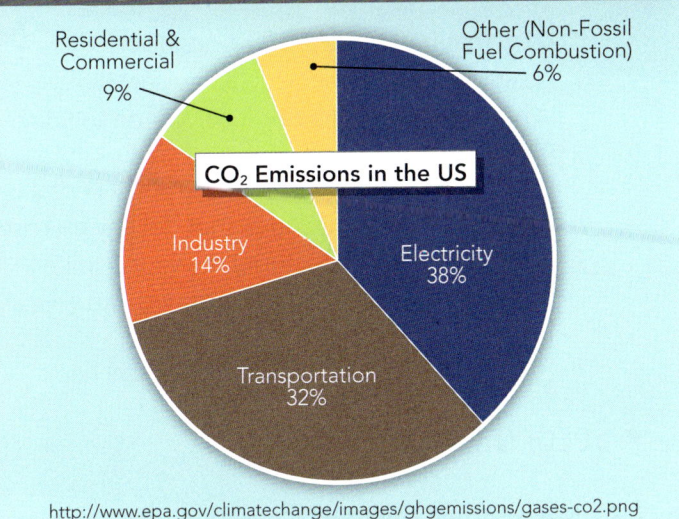

CO_2 Emissions in the US
- Residential & Commercial 9%
- Other (Non-Fossil Fuel Combustion) 6%
- Industry 14%
- Electricity 38%
- Transportation 32%

http://www.epa.gov/climatechange/images/ghgemissions/gases-co2.png

CO_2 is produced when fossil fuels are burned. The average person in the United States causes 17.6 metric tons of carbon dioxide emissions every year (see chart). The world average is 4.95 metric tons. If our emissions continue, many islands and lowland areas might disappear under the ocean, many parts of the world might become desert, and the plants and animals that live in the oceans and on ice might die.

CO_2 is absorbed by trees and changed into oxygen. However, the average tree absorbs only 10 kg of CO_2 in a year. We would need 1,760 trees per person to absorb all our CO_2 emissions, but there are only 59 trees per person in the world. Every year 25 million trees are cut down, and only 3.4 million trees are planted.

The average modern car produces 15% less CO_2 than a car that was built 10 years ago. Many new water heaters, computers and other machines also produce less CO_2 than older designs. But we use more hot water, drive farther and switch on our machines for longer each year, so we are producing more CO_2, not less.

Key Words

atmosphere	greenhouse gas
absorb	infrared radiation
fossil fuel	emission
heater	

Reading

1 Read the text and look at the chart. Are the statements true (T) or false (F)?
3.39

1 Americans cause more CO_2 emissions than the world average. T
2 Industry causes more CO_2 emissions than transportation.
3 Trees change CO_2 into oxygen.
4 There are more people in the world than trees.
5 New car designs produce more CO_2 than old ones.
6 We produce less CO_2 than we did in the past.

2 Liam is giving a presentation to his class.
3.40 Listen and match his notes (1–4) to a–d.

What could I do to produce less CO_2 when I travel?
1 My car's emissions:
2 If I rode my bike to soccer practice:
3 If we took three friends to school in our car:
4 If I got up early on Mondays:

a 1.6 kg less CO_2 per week
b 15 kg less CO_2 per week
c 600 g less CO_2 per week
d 200 g of CO_2 per km

My Science File

3 Find out what you can do to produce less CO_2 in one of these areas.
- around the house
- communication
- entertainment
- food
- travel

4 Prepare a presentation for the class, giving your ideas for producing less CO_2. Then give your presentation.

Unit 9 • Inventions 107

Review 3

Grammar • Be going to

1 Make questions and answers.

1. What / you / do / next weekend?
   What are you going to do next weekend?
2. I / play tennis.
3. Karen / clean the house.
4. Jo and Ross / do judo.
5. They / not / do any housework.
6. Maria / not / study.
7. What / Mom / make for dinner?
8. She / not / cook.
9. We / go out / for dinner!
10. you / have a pizza?

• *Will* or *be going to*

2 Complete the sentences with *will* or *be going to*.

1. I've decided what to give Mom for her birthday. I*'m going to* buy her some flowers.
2. It …. rain, I think. Look at those clouds.
3. **A** Do you think you …. be famous one day?
4. **B** Yes! Because I …. be a really successful pop singer!
5. **A** Where …. to go for summer vacation?
6. **B** I …. go to Thailand.
7. **A** How …. I know when you get there?
8. **B** I …. send you a text message!
9. **A** The menu looks good. Have you decided what you …. have?
10. **B** Hmm. I think I …. have the chicken pot pie.

• First conditional

3 Complete the First conditional sentences. Use the correct form of the verbs.

1. If I*'m* (be) free tonight, I*'ll call* (call) you.
2. I …. (give) him the message if I …. (see) him.
3. What …. (happen) if you …. (be) sick on the day of the exam?
4. If it …. (rain), we …. (not sit) outside at the restaurant.
5. You …. (not get) fit if you …. (not do) any exercise.
6. I …. (text) you if you …. (give) me your number.
7. Where …. (you go) if you …. (not get) into your first-choice college?
8. I'm sure she …. (help) you if you …. (ask) her.

• Second conditional

4 Make Second conditional questions and answers.

1. What / you do / if you / see / someone stealing?
   What would you do if you saw someone stealing?
2. If I / see someone stealing / I / call the police.
3. I / lend you my bike / if I / have one.
4. If Carrie / work harder / she / pass her exams.
5. If you / come home late, your parents / be angry?
6. I / walk away / if someone / be / rude to me.
7. If it / not raining / I / go for a walk.
8. What / you do / if you / forget / your mom's birthday?
9. If I / forget my mom's birthday / I / be sad.

• Relative pronouns

5 Complete the sentences. Use *where*, *which* or *who*.

1. These are the shoes *which* were expensive.
2. The woman …. is in the hospital is our teacher.
3. The sandwich …. I made was delicious.
4. Picasso is the artist …. painted that picture.
5. That's the café …. we go on weekends.
6. The suitcase …. is heavy is mine!
7. The dog …. barks all the time is annoying.
8. Memphis is the city …. we saw a basketball game.

Present simple passive

6 Complete the sentences with the Present simple passive form of the verbs in parentheses.

1 Every day, millions of text messages *are sent*. (send)
2 The winners .... after the contest. (announce)
3 The windows .... every two months. (clean)
4 In our school, students who misbehave .... detention. (give)
5 Ice cream .... from milk. (make)
6 Every season a new football team captain .... . (choose)
7 A lot of the world's olive oil … in Spain. (produce)
8 How often .... complaints about customer service .... ? (receive)

Past simple passive

7 Make sentences in the Past simple passive.

1 When / pizzas / first / invent?
   When were pizzas first invented?
2 Where / the first Olympic Games / hold?
3 What / yo-yos / first / use for?
4 Why / the Globe Theater / rebuild?
5 The airport / close / because of bad weather.
6 The criminal / send / to prison.
7 I / give / some money for my birthday.
8 you / invite / to their wedding?

Speaking • Persuading

1 Complete the conversation with these words.

be fun	better than	~~come on~~
don't know	I'll do	sure you

A I don't feel like going to the tango dancing class tonight.
B Oh, ¹*come on*, Alice! It'll ² .... !
A I ³ .... . I'm terrible at dancing.
B I'm ⁴ .... aren't. Anyway, we're all beginners. Please come. It'll be ⁵ .... staying at home all alone.
A OK. ⁶ .... it. Just don't laugh at me when I fall!

Talking about health

2 Put the conversation in the correct order.

.... No, I'm fine. I'll just rest here for a little while.
1 Oww!
.... I can see that by the way you're walking … Here, sit down for a second. How does that feel?
.... What's the matter, Rosie?
.... A little better, thanks.
.... Maybe you sprained it. Should I call the doctor?
.... I have a pain in my knee all of a sudden.

Problems with machines

3 Make the conversation.

1 A I / borrow your digital camera?
   Can I borrow your digital camera?
2 B Sorry, / it / not / work.
3 A What / problem / with it?
4 B There / might / something / wrong / battery.
5 A you / check / it?
6 B Yes, I / have.
7 A you / try / take / it out? And putting it back in again?
8 B No, I / haven't. I / try / that now.

Review 3 109

Review 3

Vocabulary • Protest and support

1 Choose the correct option.

1. Please sign our *banner / petition*. We are collecting signatures of people who are against the proposed new freeway.
2. The roads are closed because of a large student *demonstration / donation*.
3. We are making *signs / charities* to hold up when we go on the *sit-in / march* through the streets.
4. The *slogan / collection* of our protest movement is, "Do you call this progress?"
5. We're organizing a *sit-in / fundraising event* for a *banner / charity* called Children in Need.
6. We need people to distribute pamphlets about our organization. Would you like to be a *sign / volunteer*?
7. Please make a generous *slogan / donation* to our *collection / petition* for blind people.

• Verb + preposition

2 Complete the sentences with the correct prepositions.

1. I'm sorry, I don't agree *with* you.
2. Do you care …. the environment?
3. The government insists …. going ahead with its plans for a new airport.
4. I apologize …. my late arrival.
5. Do you ever worry …. the future?
6. What are the students protesting …. ?
7. We all hope …. a solution to the problem of global warming.
8. Do you argue …. your parents about grades?

• Extreme adjectives

3 Complete the sentences with extreme adjectives.

1. It wasn't just small—it was *tiny*.
2. It was really cold—…. , in fact.
3. We weren't just tired after the hike. We were …. .
4. The movie was more than good. It was …. .
5. It wasn't just scary—it was …. .
6. Bad? It was much worse than that. It was absolutely …. .

• Illness and injury

4 Choose the correct option.

1. I ate too much, and now I have a *sprained ankle / stomachache*.
2. I need to go the dentist. I have a *toothache / headache*.
3. Look at these spots all over my arms. It's some kind of *cough / rash*.
4. Your *burn / fever* is very high—look, it shows 39°C on the thermometer.
5. I have a *backache / sore throat*—it really hurts when I eat.
6. I have a bad *cold / cut* on my finger. It's bleeding a lot.

• Machine nouns and verbs

5 Choose the correct option.

1. *Plug / Attach* the machine into the outlet.
2. *Attach / Press* the cord to the back of the machine.
3. *Produce / Press* the button to start the machine.
4. Do you know how energy is *communicated / produced*?
5. We usually *invent / communicate* by email or text.
6. You should always *plug in / turn off* machines when they aren't in use.

• Word building

6 Complete the text with the correct form of the words.

The ¹*inventors* (invent) of the first hot-air balloon were the Montgolfier brothers. They ² …. (build) the balloon in 1793. The idea for the ³ …. (invent) came when they burned some paper. The fire ⁴ …. (product) hot air, which made the paper float up into the air. Later, they ⁵ …. (designer) a balloon from cloth and paper. They made a fire under it. The first passengers were a duck, a sheep and a chicken.

Word list

Unit 7 • Make a Difference

Protest and support

banner	/ˈbænɚ/
charity	/ˈtʃærəti/
collection	/kəˈlɛkʃən/
demonstration	/ˌdɛmənˈstreɪʃən/
donation	/doʊˈneɪʃən/
fundraising event	/ˈfʌndreɪzɪŋ ɪˌvɛnt/
march (n)	/mɑrtʃ/
petition (n)	/pəˈtɪʃən/
sign (n)	/saɪn/
sit-in (n)	/ˈsɪt ɪn/
slogan	/ˈsloʊgən/
volunteer (n)	/ˌvɑlənˈtɪr/

Verb + preposition

agree with	/əˈgri wɪð, wɪθ/
apologize for	/əˈpɑləˌdʒaɪz fɚ, fɔr/
argue with	/ˈɑrgyu wɪð, wɪθ/
believe in	/bəˈliv ɪn/
care about	/ˈkɛr əˌbaʊt/
decide on	/dɪˈsaɪd ɔn/
disapprove of	/ˌdɪsəˈpruv əv/
hope for	/ˈhoʊp fɚ, fɔr/
insist on	/ɪnˈsɪst ɔn, ɑn/
know about	/ˈnoʊ əˌbaʊt/
protest about	/ˈproʊtɛst əˌbaʊt/
worry about	/ˈwɚi, ˈwʌri əˌbaʊt/

Unit 8 • Danger and Risk

Extreme adjectives

awful	/ˈɔfəl/
burning	/ˈbɚnɪŋ/
excellent	/ˈɛksələnt/
exhausted	/ɪgˈzɔstɪd/
freezing	/ˈfrizɪŋ/
furious	/ˈfyʊriəs/
huge	/hyudʒ/
terrifying	/ˈtɛrəˌfaɪ-ɪŋ/
thrilled	/θrɪld/
tiny	/ˈtaɪni/

Illness and injury

a backache	/ˈbækeɪk/
a burn	/bɚn/
a cold	/koʊld/
a cough	/kɔf/
a cut	/kʌt/
a fever	/ˈfivɚ/
a headache	/ˈhɛdeɪk/
a rash	/ræʃ/
a sore throat	/ˌsɔr ˈθroʊt/
a sprained ankle	/ˌspreɪnd ˈæŋkəl/
a stomachache	/ˈstʌmək-eɪk/
a toothache	/ˈtuθeɪk/

Unit 9 • Inventions

Machine verbs

attach	/əˈtætʃ/
build	/bɪld/
communicate	/kəˈmyunəˌkeɪt/
invent	/ɪnˈvɛnt/
plug in	/ˌplʌg ˈɪn/
press	/prɛs/
produce	/prəˈdus/
turn off	/ˌtɚn ˈɔf/
turn on	/ˌtɚn ˈɔn/

Machine nouns

battery	/ˈbætəri/
button	/ˈbʌtn/
cable	/ˈkeɪbəl/
jack	/dʒæk/
keyboard	/ˈkibɔrd/
outlet	/ˈaʊtˌlɛt/
power cord	/ˌpaʊɚ ˈkɔrd/
remote control	/rɪˌmoʊt kənˈtroʊl/
tube	/tub/
wheel	/wil/

Word building

build	/bɪld/
builder	/ˈbɪldɚ/
building	/ˈbɪldɪŋ/
design	/dɪˈzaɪn/
designer	/dɪˈzaɪnɚ/
design	/dɪˈzaɪn/
invent	/ɪnˈvɛnt/
inventor	/ɪnˈvɛntɚ/
invention	/ɪnˈvɛnʃən/
paint	/peɪnt/
painter	/ˈpeɪntɚ/
painting	/ˈpeɪntɪŋ/
produce	/prəˈdus/
producer	/prəˈdusɚ/
product	/ˈprɑdʌkt/
write	/raɪt/
writer	/ˈraɪtɚ/
writing	/ˈraɪtɪŋ/

Brain Trainers

Unit 1
Find the difference

1. Look at the photo on page 14 for one minute. Now study this photo. What differences can you find?

Vocabulary

2a. Find the word that doesn't belong in each box. You have one minute.

wa**l**l   roof   ceiling
garage   **f**loor

attic   stai**r**s
hallway   basement   offic**e**

lan**d**ing   yard   bal**c**ony
patio   driv**e**way

2b. Arrange the letters in bold to make a new home word.

3. Look at the objects in the grid for one minute. Cover the grid and write the words in your notebook. How many objects can you remember?

Unit 2
Find the difference

1. Look at the photo on page 24 for one minute. Now study this photo. What differences can you find?

Brain Trainers

Vocabulary

2 Make words. Each word has three shapes.

inte-rest-ing

inte	or	tic
dra	ri	ing
col	rest	ful
hor	ma	ble

3 Work in pairs. Say an adjective. Your partner says the adjective and correct preposition. Then switch roles.

proud	angry	bad	tired
excited	bored	sorry	interested
good	afraid	popular	

> proud

> proud of

Unit 3
Find the difference

1 Look at the photo on page 34 for one minute. Now study this photo. What differences can you find?

Vocabulary

2 Work in pairs. Student A chooses a shopping word. Student B asks Student A the questions below. Student B guesses the word.

coin bargain salesperson line price *change* product *vendor* *customers*

Questions
How many syllables are there?
How many letters are there?
How many vowels are there?

> How many letters are there?

> Seven.

3a Complete the five pairs of money verbs below. You have one minute.

b_y   s_ _l
s_ v_   sp_ _d
w_n   e_ _n
c_ s_   _ff_ _ d
l_ _d   b_ _ r_ w

3b Complete the sentence with two money phrases.

You can pay for things in c_ _h or by c_ _ _ _ t c _ _ _ .

Brain Trainers 113

Brain Trainers

Unit 4

Find the difference

1. Look at the photo on page 48 for one minute. Now study this photo. What differences can you find?

Vocabulary

2. How many *news* words can you think of in one minute? Try to remember at least seven.

   1 local news

3a. Read the pairs of words aloud three times. Cover them and read the list below. Which word is missing?

   quietly → loudly   carefully → carelessly
   happily → sadly   patiently → angrily

   | carefully | angrily | loudly | happily |
   | quietly | patiently | carelessly | |

3b. Now make more adverbs using the different colored letters. Then match the opposites.

   well – badly

Unit 5

Find the difference

1. Look at the photo on page 58 for one minute. Now study this photo. What differences can you find?

Vocabulary

2. Look at the pictures for two minutes. Try to remember them in order. Then cover them. Take turns making suggestions. Can you remember all nine?

114 Brain Trainers

Brain Trainers

3a Find six meanings for the verb *get* in the puzzle. You have two minutes.

3b Think of one more meaning for the verb *get*.

b	g	h	s	p	n	r
b	r	i	n	g	r	e
e	a	b	m	i	d	c
c	l	u	o	c	r	e
o	h	y	v	y	k	i
m	u	r	e	n	e	v
e	a	r	r	i	v	e

Unit 6
Find the difference

1 Look at the photo on page 68 for one minute. Now study this photo. What differences can you find?

Vocabulary

2 Work in small groups. Choose an activity from the box. Act it out. Your classmates guess the activity.

- do the dishes
- feed the cat
- set the table
- mow the lawn
- do the ironing
- make the bed
- cook a meal
- do the laundry
- wash the car
- sweep the floor

3 Look at the faces carefully. Match them with the feelings adjectives. Write the answers in your notebook. Then check your answers on page 117.

> relaxed   confused   nervous   upset
> confident   disappointed   embarrassed   fed up

1 *fed up*

Brain Trainers

Unit 7

Find the difference

1. Look at the photo on page 82 for one minute. Now study this photo. What differences can you find?

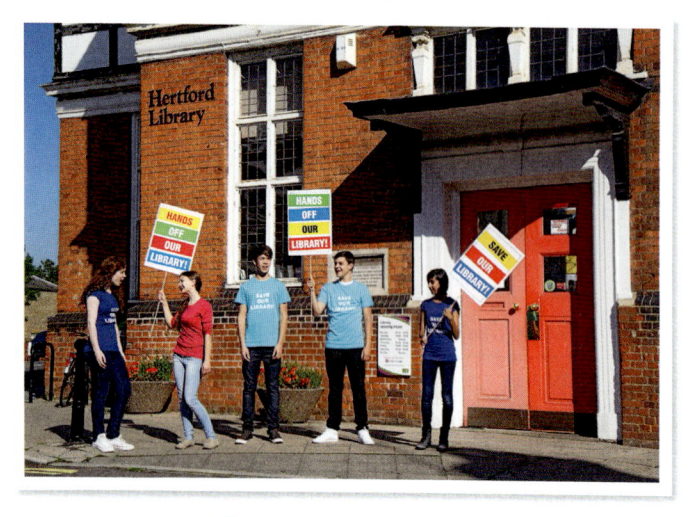

Vocabulary

2. How many protest words and phrases can you think of with the letter *n* in them? Think of ten.

   a banner

3. Read the phrases for two minutes. Cover the list and write the phrases in your notebook. How many can you remember?

care about	argue with
hope for	apologize for
decide on	worry about
disapprove of	agree with
know about	believe in
protest against	insist on

Unit 8

Find the difference

1. Look at the photo on page 92 for one minute. Now study this photo. What differences can you find?

Vocabulary

2. Look at the photos. Use an extreme adjective to describe each one. You have two minutes.

   1 *huge*

   Which two extreme adjectives are missing?

Brain Trainers

3 Work in small groups. Choose an illness or injury. Act it out. Your classmates guess the problem.

> Do you have a cut on your hand?

> No.

> Do you have a burn?

> Yes, I do!

Unit 9
Find the difference

1 Look at the photo on page 102 for one minute. Now study this photo. What differences can you find?

Vocabulary

2a Read the colored words and phrases aloud three times. Cover them and read the list below. Which word was missing?

cable   button   communicate
plug in   press   turn on   keyboard

| plug in | outlet | press | button |
| turn on | keyboard | cable | communicate |

2b Now try again.

attach   remote control   tube
battery   wheel   invent   build

| invent | wheel | build | battery |
| attach | tube | turn off | remote control |

3a Make words. Each word has three shapes.

in-ven-tor

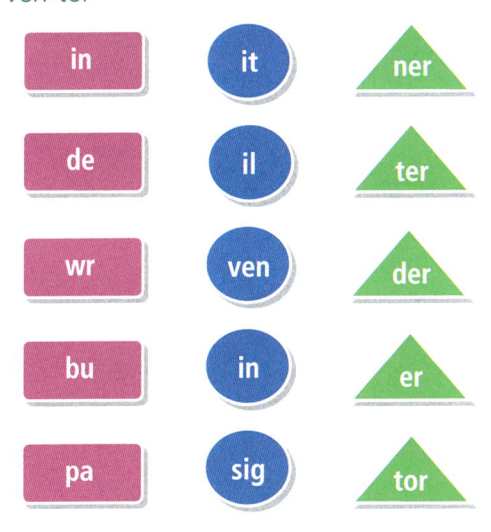

in	it	ner
de	il	ter
wr	ven	der
bu	in	er
pa	sig	tor

3b Now say what each person does. What is the result of their work?

> An inventor ....

> The result is ....

Answers to Brain Trainers Unit 6 Exercise 3
1 fed up 2 confident 3 embarrassed 4 relaxed
5 confused 6 upset 7 disappointed 8 nervous

Brain Trainers 117

Listening Bank

Unit 1

1 **Listen again. Listen to the description of Hannah's
1.11** **room and what that says about her personality.**

pale walls – talkative

2 **Listen again. Complete the sentences.**
1.11
1 Hannah's walls are pale *yellow*.
2 There's a bright green …. on the bed.
3 She …. trying new things.
4 She has pictures of …. and friends on the walls.
5 Her room is pretty …. at the moment.
6 Her …. likes cleaning up in her room.

Unit 2

1 **Listen again. Choose the correct option.**
1.24
1 The picture is *real / fake*.
2 The men were *240 / 3,300* meters above the streets.
3 The men were working in *Slovakia / America*.
4 Gusti Popovic is the man *on the right / on the left*.
5 He sent *a letter / a postcard* with the photo.
6 Gusti Popovic was *good at / bad at* his job.

2 **Listen again. Answer the questions.**
1.24
1 Does the boy think the photo is real at first?
No, he doesn't.
2 What does the girl say about Charles Ebbets?
3 What does the boy ask about the men?
4 How does the girl identify Gusti Popovic?
5 Does she say he sent his wife a photo?

Unit 3

1 **Listen again. What do these numbers refer to?**
1.36
1 16 *the age of the boy*
2 $95
3 2
4 20
5 65,000

2 **Listen again and complete the sentences.**
1.36
1 The boy bought a *console* and two games online.
2 The console arrived in the …. .
3 There were a lot of 20-dollar …. in the box.
4 The boy and his parents talked to the …. .
5 They were worried the money came from …. .
6 The police want to find the owner of the …. .

Unit 4

1 **Listen. Match the speakers (1–3) to the opinions
2.11** **(a–c).**

Speaker 1
Speaker 2
Speaker 3
a I'm not interested in international news. It's not important to me.
b The news is always bad. It's about wars or natural disasters.
c It's good to know what's happening in the world.

2 **Listen again. Choose the correct options.**
2.11
1 Speaker 1 *has read / hasn't read* the news today.
2 He *sometimes / often* reads his dad's newspaper.
3 He *has / doesn't have* time to read the newspaper every day.
4 Speaker 2 listened to the news *on the radio / on TV*.
5 She thinks there was a headline about a *politicians / world leaders* meeting.
6 She *can / can't* remember all of today's headlines.
7 Speaker 3 read the headlines *in a newspaper / on a news website*.
8 The Yankees are playing the Red Sox next *month / week*.
9 Speaker 3 is interested in *the sports section / general news*.

Listening Bank

Unit 5

1 **Listen. Choose the correct answers.**
2.22
1 Which country did Troy just visit?
   a *Fiji*
   b Japan
   c Turkey
2 What can you do in the first hotel?
   a open the windows
   b feed the fish
   c go swimming
3 What can you find in the second hotel?
   a an alarm clock
   b big windows
   c a large bed
4 What are rooms at the third hotel like?
   a dark and wet
   b warm and comfortable
   c very small
5 Which place does Troy recommend for a vacation?
   a Fiji
   b Japan
   c Turkey

2 **Listen again. Answer the questions.**
2.22
1 Where was the hotel in Fiji?
   25 meters under the sea
2 What does each room in the hotel have?
3 What's unusual about the hotel in Japan?
4 Are there any beds in the hotel?
5 Where is the hotel in Cappadocia?
6 Why does Troy recommend Cappadocia for a vacation?

Cappadocia

Unit 6

1 **Listen again. Choose the correct options.**
2.35
Conversation 1
1 The boy thinks the girl should wear
   a pants.   b shorts.   c *a dress*.
2 The girl can't wear this because it's
   a not small enough.   b too small.   c horrible.

Conversation 2
3 The boy has to
   a clear the table.
   b hang out laundry.
   c set the table.
4 The boy is feeling
   a grateful.   b glad.   c fed up.

Conversation 3
5 The boy wants to go to a party with
   a robots.   b football players.   c his mom.
6 He can't go to the party because it's too
   a late.   b expensive.   c far away.

Conversation 4
7 The girl is having problems with
   a her English.   b her computer.   c her math.
8 The boy thinks she should
   a learn from him.
   b learn from his teacher.
   c become a teacher.

Listening Bank 119

Listening Bank

Unit 7

1 Listen again. Complete the information pamphlet.
3.9

Family Shoebox Appeal

How to prepare a box

1. Choose a ¹ *shoebox*.
2. Fill ² .... with gifts.
3. Put ³ .... in the box. This pays for shipping.
4. Take your box to the Shoebox collection point.

What's in a box?
- things for ⁴ .... , e.g., notebooks, pencils
- other useful things: a toothbrush, ⁵ ....

Don't put in
- medicine, ⁶ .... or scissors.

Unit 8

1 Listen again. Choose the correct options to complete the advertisement.
3.23

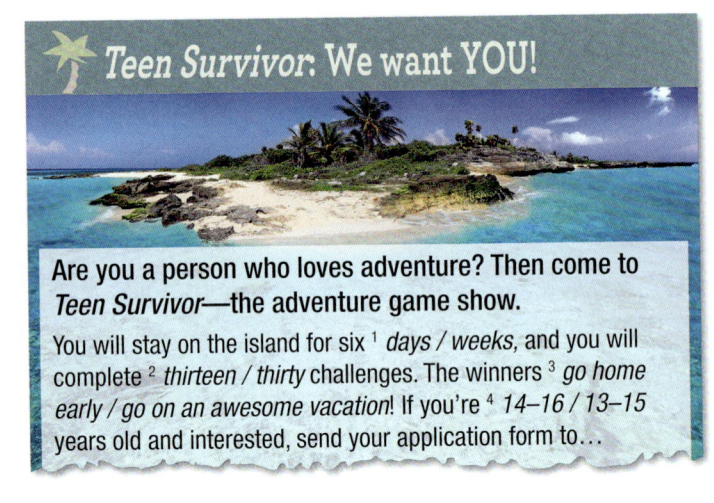

Teen Survivor: We want YOU!

Are you a person who loves adventure? Then come to *Teen Survivor*—the adventure game show.

You will stay on the island for six ¹ *days / weeks,* and you will complete ² *thirteen / thirty* challenges. The winners ³ *go home early / go on an awesome vacation*! If you're ⁴ *14–16 / 13–15* years old and interested, send your application form to…

2 Listen again. Are these statements true (T) or false (F)?
3.23
1. The girl saw an announcement in a magazine. *F*
2. The girl and boy both watch the show.
3. The show is on a desert island.
4. The boy is worried about the challenges.
5. The girl is interested in the prize.
6. They can both apply for the show.

Unit 9

1 Listen to the conversation. What advantages and disadvantages of reading on a smart phone did the speakers mention?
3.36

2 Listen again. Are these statements true (T) or false (F)?
3.36
1. The boy read a horror story on his smart phone. *F*
2. The boy reads at the bus stop.
3. He likes carrying books with him because they're small.
4. The girl thinks smart phone screens are a good size for reading.
5. The boy has thirteen e-books on his smart phone.
6. The girl likes keeping her books for years.

3 Correct the false statements from Exercise 2.

1. *The boy read a science fiction story on his smart phone.*

Culture 1 Homes in the US

Reading

1 Read about Homes in the US. Why are detached houses often located in the suburbs?
3.41

2 Read about Homes in the US again. Are the statements true (T) or false (F)? Correct the false statements.
1 Row houses usually have a big yard.
2 Sixty-four percent of homes in the US are detached houses.
3 There are more homes in large apartment buildings than there are mobile homes in the US.
4 There are a lot of large apartment buildings in cities.

Your Culture

3 In pairs, answer the questions.
1 In your area, what type of home do most people live in?
2 Which of these things are common in homes in your area?
 • an attic   • a balcony   • a basement
 • a garage   • a yard
3 Think of another part of your country. What types of homes are popular there?
4 Are there many very tall buildings in big cities? Are they homes, offices or both?

4 Write a short paragraph about homes in your country. Use your answers to Exercise 3 and the Homes in the US examples to help you.

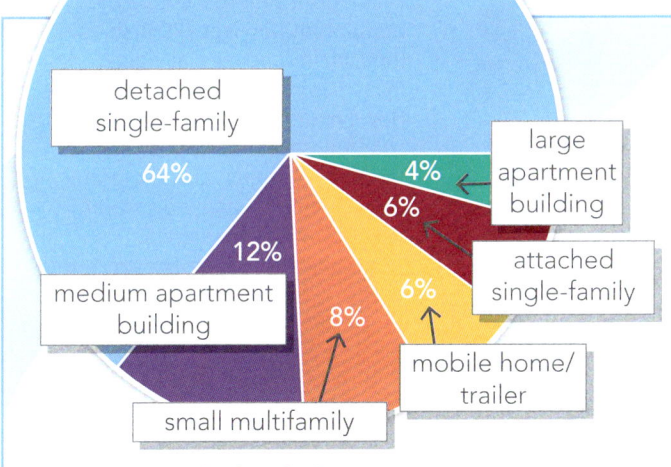

Types of Homes in the US

- detached single-family 64%
- medium apartment building 12%
- small multifamily 8%
- mobile home/trailer 6%
- attached single-family 6%
- large apartment building 4%

Detached single-family houses
Detached single-family houses are separate buildings usually surrounded by a yard. They are the most common type of house in the US. Single-family homes often include a garage. They come in a few different architectural styles, depending on the region of the country. They are often located in American suburbs, where larger lots of land and fewer people per square kilometer allow for this type of house.

Row houses
There are a few different types of attached single-family houses in the US: row houses, townhomes and duplexes are the primary types. They share at least one wall and are often found in semiurban or urban areas. They often include a patio or small yard in the back, and sometimes have a garage or driveway for parking.

Small/medium multifamily houses
One-fifth of the housing units in the US are small (2–4 units) to medium (5–49 units) multifamily buildings or apartment buildings and complexes. Each unit could be as small as a studio apartment or could include three to four bedrooms.

Large apartment buildings
Large apartment buildings with more than 50 units are more common in US cities. Some apartments have balconies, and buildings often include one or more shared facilities.

Mobile homes or trailers
Mobile homes are an inexpensive form of housing in the US. People often rent a small space in an area of land, called a trailer park, to set up their mobile home and connect it to city facilities, like water and sewer.

Culture 2 The Republic of Ireland

Reading

1 Read about the Republic of Ireland. Which of
3.42 these things are mentioned?

| business | dancing | mountains | religion |
| technology | tradition | TV | |

2 Read about the Republic of Ireland again and choose the correct options.
1 *All / Some* of Ireland is in the United Kingdom.
2 Irish is the main language in *some / all* schools in Ireland.
3 In Irish dancing, you move your *feet / arms*.
4 Some people say that *not many / many* Irish people talk a lot.

Your Culture

3 In pairs, answer the questions.
1 Was your country ever ruled by another country? Which one? Did this change your language or other parts of your culture?
2 What type of dancing is your country famous for? Have you ever tried it?
3 Is there anywhere in your country that has a strange tradition? What is it?

4 Write a short paragraph about your country. Use your answers to Exercise 3 and the Republic of Ireland examples to help you.

THE REPUBLIC OF IRELAND

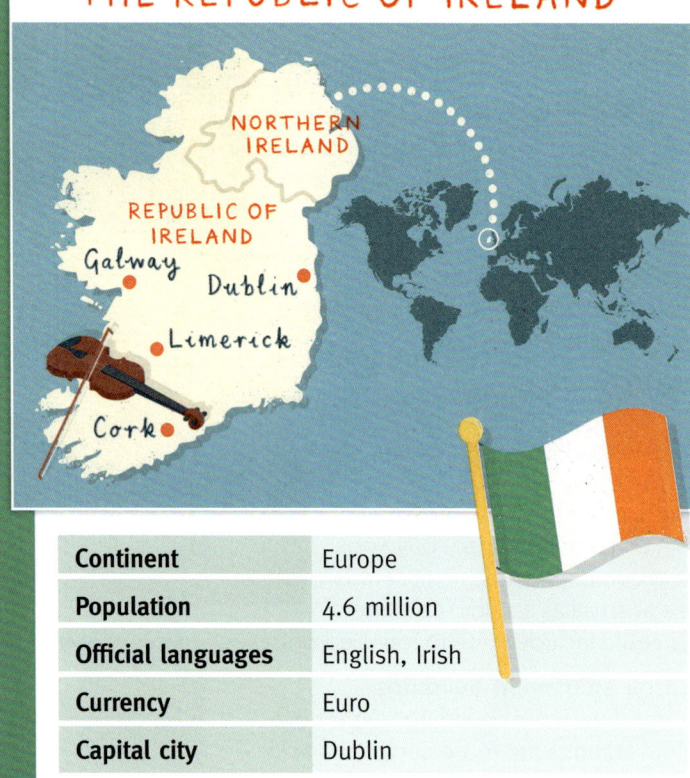

Continent	Europe
Population	4.6 million
Official languages	English, Irish
Currency	Euro
Capital city	Dublin

North and South
For many centuries Ireland was ruled by the English, but in the early twentieth century, most of the island became an independent country, the Republic of Ireland. Northern Ireland, however, continued to be part of the United Kingdom. The two parts of Ireland have a shared culture, but there are some religious differences. In the north, most people are Protestants; in the south, most people are Catholics.

This is a shamrock, the symbol of Ireland

Language
Only about one percent of the population now speaks Irish as their main language at home. Most people speak English. However, more and more children are going to Irish-speaking schools, and there are several Irish TV channels, radio stations and newspapers.

Culture
Ireland has a strong cultural influence on the English-speaking world. It has produced many great writers, including Oscar Wilde and George Bernard Shaw; actors, including Pierce Brosnan and Colin Farrell; and musicians, including U2. Irish step dancing—fast foot movements while the body and arms don't move—has also become popular around the world.

The Gift of Gab
At Blarney Castle in the south of Ireland, you can find the Blarney Stone. According to tradition, if you kiss this special stone you will have the "gift of gab"—the ability to talk well and persuade people easily. Some people think that the Irish are the most talkative people in the world. Have they all kissed the Blarney Stone?

Culture 3 — Sports in the UK

Reading

1 Read about Sports in the UK.
3.43 Which sport

1. is the UK's favorite?
2. is popular in the summer?
3. is popular with older people?
4. shares its name with a school?

2 Read about Sports in the UK again. Answer the questions.

1. How long are the longest cricket games?
2. In soccer, what important things happened in the UK before they happened in other countries?
3. What three differences are there between soccer and rugby?
4. Why did the king make playing golf illegal?

Your Culture

3 In pairs, answer the questions.

1. Are any of the sports on this page popular in your country? Which ones? Are you a fan of these sports?
2. What sports started in your country? Do you like playing or watching them?
3. What are the most important sports events in your country? Where and when do they happen?

4 Write a short paragraph about sports in your country. Use your answers to Exercise 3 and the Sports in the UK examples to help you.

SPORTS in the UK

Cricket
Cricket began in England about four hundred years ago. Today, there are cricket games all over the country on summer weekends. A local game takes all afternoon. Professional games at famous stadiums, like Lord's in London, can last for five days, and there is often no winner at the end. People play cricket in most English-speaking countries, and it is very popular in India and Pakistan.

Soccer
The UK was the first country in the world with international soccer teams, professional players and a national soccer tournament. Today soccer is the UK's most popular sport, and the English Premier League has some of the world's most famous clubs and players. The most important game of the year is the FA Cup Final at London's Wembley Stadium.

Rugby
This sport began in Rugby School, a famous English school. It is like soccer, but there are some big differences. The ball is an oval shape, and you can carry it as well as kick it. You can also pull players off their feet. Every year there is an important tournament, the Six Nations, between the teams of England, Scotland, Wales, Ireland, France and Italy.

Golf
Golf began in Scotland. In the fifteenth century, the sport was illegal— the king was worried that it was taking too much of people's time. Later, the sport became popular around the world. Many older people play golf in the UK today, and some of the best professional players are British.

Culture 4 Robin Hood

Reading

1 Read about Robin Hood. Are these descriptions true (T), false (F) or don't know (DK)?

- a character in TV shows
- a hero
- a king
- a real thief
- the Sheriff of Nottingham

2 Read about Robin Hood again. Answer the questions.

1 Why did Robin Hood go to the Middle East?
2 Why did he and his friends steal money?
3 How long have there been stories about Robin Hood?
4 Why do people visit the Major Oak?

Your Culture

3 In pairs, answer the questions.

1 What traditional heroes are there in your culture?
2 What do they do in the stories about them?
3 Are the stories true?

4 Write a short paragraph about traditional heroes in your country. Use your answers to Exercise 3 and the Robin Hood examples to help you.

Robin Hood

The Major Oak

A statue of Robin Hood in Nottingham

Robin Hood is England's most famous hero. What do we know about him?

The stories
Robin was a rich man from the north of England. He was very good at archery and went to the Middle East to fight with King Richard I. When he came home, the Sheriff of Nottingham took his lands, so he lived in Sherwood Forest with a group of friends—Little John, Will Scarlett and others. They stole money from the rich and gave it to the poor.

Are the stories true?
We don't know. There are a lot of old documents about the thieves at the end of the twelfth century, when Richard I was king. But no one has found documents about a Robin Hood in Nottingham.

Robin Hood today
Robin Hood has been the hero of songs and stories for more than six hundred years, and there have been more than fifty films and TV shows about him. There is a big Robin Hood celebration in Nottingham every year. People wear twelfth-century clothes, listen to stories and music and try archery. They also go to the Robin Hood Visitor Center in Sherwood Forest and see a big, old tree known as the Major Oak. In some stories, Robin hid from the Sheriff's men inside it.

Russell Crowe as Robin Hood in the 2010 movie

Culture 5 — Multicultural America

Reading

1 Read about Multicultural America. Match the different groups of people (1–4) to these things.
3.45

| Chinatown | civil rights | Hawaii |
| jazz | newspapers | two percent |

2 Read about Multicultural America again. Complete the sentences.
1 Five percent of the people in the US are …. .
2 You can buy Spanish …. and hear Spanish radio in American cities.
3 African Americans fought for …. and …. rights throughout American history.
4 People with parents from different ethnic groups are called …. .

Your Culture

3 In pairs, answer the questions.
1 What ethnic groups are there in your country?
2 How long have they lived there?
3 What other countries' food is popular in your country?
4 Are there many immigrants in your country? Where do many people emigrate from?

4 Write a short paragraph about different cultures in your country. Use your answers to Exercise 3 and the Multicultural America examples to help you.

Multicultural America

Many groups of people have come to the land inhabited by Native American tribes, now known as the United States of America. The following are some important racial and ethnic groups in the United States.

1 African American
Africans were brought to North America as slaves by Europeans when the land was colonized by the British and the French in the seventeenth century. African Americans now make up 13 percent of the population. Many of the best-known aspects of American culture, such as jazz, rock and hip hop music, come from African American culture. The African Americans' fight for freedom and civil rights has defined American history.

2 Hispanic or Latino
The land that is now Texas, California and the American Southwest belonged to Mexico until the mid-nineteenth century. People from all the Central and South American countries continue to migrate to the United States, increasing the Latino community. Overall, 17 percent of the US population is Hispanic. Latinos are also the fastest-growing group. Spanish is the second most commonly spoken language in the US after English, and Spanish-language newspapers, radio stations and TV channels are widely available. Food from Latin American countries, especially Mexico, is also very popular in the US.

3 Asian and Pacific Islander
Asians (including South Asians) and native Hawaiians, along with other Pacific Islanders, make up 5 percent of the US population, with significant communities on both the East and West Coasts. Every major city has its "Chinatown," a predominantly Asian neighborhood. The two most famous Chinatowns are in San Francisco and New York City. People in the US enjoy Asian and South Asian foods, especially Chinese, Japanese and Indian food.

4 Mixed race
Two percent of American children are mixed race—their parents come from different ethnic groups.

Culture 6 Canada

Reading

1 Read about Canada. What is the most important language in each region?
3.46
1 Ontario
2 Quebec
3 Nunavut

2 Read about Canada again. Complete the sentences with place names.
1 The capital city of Canada is …. .
2 Niagara Falls is a popular place for visitors in the …. region.
3 A lot of maple syrup comes from …. .
4 People in the town of …. don't see the sun for four months in winter.

Your Culture

3 In pairs, answer the questions.
1 What are the most popular places in your country for visitors from other countries?
2 Are there regions in your country where the country's official language isn't the principal language? Do people in these regions want to be independent? Give examples.
3 What food is your country or region famous for?
4 Are there any regions where few people live? Why don't more people live there?

4 Write a short paragraph about different regions in your country. Use your answers to Exercise 3 and the Canada examples to help you.

CANADA

Continent	North America
Population	35 million
Official languages	English, French
Currency	Canadian dollar
Favorite sport	Ice hockey

Canada is the world's second-largest country, but a lot of the land in the center and north is uninhabited. Canada is famous for its cold winters and beautiful mountains.

Ontario
Canada's biggest city, Toronto, and its capital, Ottawa, are in this region. Here, as in most of Canada, English is the principal language. A lot of people come here to visit Niagara Falls and the Great Lakes.

Quebec
Canada's second-biggest city, Montreal, is here. Most people in Quebec speak French, and about 40 percent want Quebec to be an independent country. The majority of Canada's maple syrup comes from Quebec. Canadians eat this delicious syrup with pancakes, and the leaf of the maple tree even appears on their flag.

Nunavut
Nunavut is the biggest region in Canada, yet only 33,000 people live there. There are no trees, and the land and sea are frozen for most of the year. It is easier to travel by snowmobile than by car. At Grise Fiord, the farthest north of Nunavut's towns, people endure four months without daylight in winter and four months without night in summer. Most people in Nunavut are Inuit. They speak the Inuit language, but they don't live in igloos. They have houses with TVs and Internet.

Irregular Verb List

Verb	Past Simple	Past Participle
be	was/were	been
become	became	become
begin	began	begun
break	broke	broken
bring	brought	brought
build	built	built
buy	bought	bought
can	could	been able
catch	caught	caught
choose	chose	chosen
come	came	come
cost	cost	cost
cut	cut	cut
do	did	done
draw	drew	drawn
drink	drank	drunk
drive	drove	driven
eat	ate	eaten
fall	fell	fallen
feed	fed	fed
feel	felt	felt
fight	fought	fought
find	found	found
fly	flew	flown
forget	forgot	forgotten
get	got	gotten
give	gave	given
go	went	gone/been
grow	grew	grown
have	had	had
hear	heard	heard
hold	held	held
keep	kept	kept
know	knew	known
leave	left	left
lend	lent	lent
light	lit	lit
lose	lost	lost
make	made	made
mean	meant	meant
meet	met	met
pay	paid	paid
put	put	put
read /riːd/	read /rɛd/	read /rɛd/
ride	rode	ridden
ring	rang	rung
run	ran	run
say	said	said
see	saw	seen
sell	sold	sold
send	sent	sent
shine	shone	shone
show	showed	shown
sing	sang	sung
sit	sat	sat
sleep	slept	slept
speak	spoke	spoken
spend	spent	spent
stand	stood	stood
steal	stole	stolen
swim	swam	swum
take	took	taken
teach	taught	taught
tell	told	told
think	thought	thought
throw	threw	thrown
understand	understood	understood
wake	woke	woken
wear	wore	worn
win	won	won
write	wrote	written

Pearson Education Limited
Edinburgh Gate
Harlow
Essex CM20 2JE
England
and Associated Companies throughout the world.

www.pearsonelt.com/moveit

© Pearson Education Limited 2015

The right of Fiona Beddall and Jayne Wildman to be identified as the authors of this work has been asserted by them in accordance with the Copyright, Designs and Patents Act, 1988.

All rights reserved. No part of this publication may be reproduced, stored in a retrieval system, or transmitted in any form or by any means, electronic, mechanical, photocopying, recording, or otherwise without the prior written permission of the Publishers.

First published 2015
Fifth impression 2017
Set in 10.5/12.5pt LTC Helvetica Neue Light
ISBN: 978-1-4479-8339-2

Acknowledgements
We are grateful to the following for permission to reproduce copyright material:
Article 1.1 adapted from www.minihousebuilder.com; Article 6.7 adapted from www.bullyingcanada.ca

In some instances we have been unable to trace the owners of copyright material and we would appreciate any information that would enable us to do so.

Photo Acknowledgements
The publisher would like to thank the following for their kind permission to reproduce their photographs:

(Key: b-bottom; c-centre; l-left; r-right; t-top)

akg-images Ltd: 104tr, Erich Lessing 104cl; **Alamy Images:** AAD Worldwide Travel Images 20tr, AE / Gunter Marx 88t, Colin Palmer Photography 124tr, Ashley Cooper 78c, CountrySideCollection - Homer Sykes 123tl, Design Pics Inc 78bl, Bert Hoferichter 126bl, imagebroker 20cl, Impressions / Balan Madhavan 79l, David L. Moore 45, Picture Contact BV 126br, Adrian Sherratt 27b, Evan Spiler 119r, ZUMA Press, Inc 79r; **Bridgeman Art Library Ltd:** Arundel Castle 104cr; **Bullying Canada:** Charles Benn 73r; **Crina Coco Popescu:** 97l, 97r; **Corbis:** Bettmann 118, Destinations 55tr, 122tr, epa / Jerry Lampen 94l, Leonard Gertz 116br/8, Simon Jarratt 27t, Minden Pictures / Foto Natura / Do Van Dijck 116br/7, Ocean 20tl, 65r, Pool / Retna Ltd 80r, Reuters / Peter Andrews 60tr, David Turnley 50; **Divine Chocolate:** 87tr, Kim Naylor 87tl; **Dynamic Graphics, Inc.:** 126tr; **Fotolia.com:** Aaron Amat 116br/6, Pablo H. Caridad 19tr, dell 72, Aleksandar Jocic 37, Patryk Kosmider 120r, Miravision 62, Monia 20bl, 42, Anna Omelchenko 116br/2, Pascal Rateau 19cr, Scanrail 105, Petr Vaclavek 104tl; **Getty Images:** 2009 Blixah 7, 36r, 78t, 78cl, 78br, 119l, 123tr, 123br, Maxine Adcock 36l, AFP 60cr, 88c, Todd Bigelow 60cl, Scott Cramer 88b, DreamPictures 47, Tony Eveling 21cl, Gamma-Rapho 53tr, 53br, Scott MacBride 20br, Regine Mahaux 12, National Geographic 99l (Bkgd), Michael Nichols 21bl, Simon Rawles 87b, Kenneth Riley 63b, Alberto E. Rodriguez 53tl, Aurora Rodriguez 21cr, Henrik Sorensen 116br/1, Time & Life Pictures 26l, Time Life Pictures 26tr, UNICEF 51, Yellow Dog Productions 71; **Pearson Education Ltd:** Gareth Boden 8, 9tl, 9tr, 9bl, 9br, 14, 24, 34, 48, 58, 68, 82, 92, 102, 112tl, 112br, 113bl, 114tl, 114tr, 115bl, 116tl, 116tr, 117l; **Press Association Images:** Demotix / Clive Chilvers 78cr, Manchester City FC / Ed Garvey 123bl; **Reuters:** Karoly Arvai 84r; **Rex Features:** 110, Albanpix Ltd 29tl, 29tr, 29b, c.Warner Br / Everett 52, Robert Harding / Charles Bowman 124tl, Geoffrey Robinson 99cl/a, The World of Sports SC 26br, Universal / Everett 124br; Jorge Rodriguez-Gerada: 84l; **Shutterstock.com:** 90, Lance Bellers 109, BestPhotoStudio 81, 108, Brandon Blinkenberg 126cr, col 121tr, Corepics VOF, Louise Cukrov 19tl, Deymos.HR 31l, Jaimie Duplass 56, K. Geijer 121bl, Warren Goldswain 55bl, gudak 99bl/b, Kamira 125c, Andrew Lam 121br, littleny 31r, Stuart Monk 125r, PhotoHouse 125l, rSnapshotPhotos 121cr, Dmitriy Shironosov 76; **SuperStock:** age fotostock / Mark Beton 61, age fotostock / Werner Otto 116br/5, Aurora Open / Tom Bol 55cr, Image Source 65l, OJO Images 116br/4, Oredia / Oredia Eurl / Antoine Juliette 116br/3, Prisma 19br, 20cr, The Irish Image Collection 122br; **The Kobal Collection:** Warner Bros 89; **TopFoto:** The Granger Collection 104br; **www.StopBullying.gov:** 73l; **www.tumbleweedhouses.com:** 11

All other images © Pearson Education

Cover image: Front: **Shutterstock.com:** Galina Barskaya

Every effort has been made to trace the copyright holders and we apologise in advance for any unintentional omissions. We would be pleased to insert the appropriate acknowledgement in any subsequent edition of this publication.

Illustrated by: Andy Robert Davies pages 10, 13, 17, 64; Paula Franco pages 4, 5, 22, 33, 44, 54, 57, 91, 114, 115; Peskimo pages 16, 30,70, 94, 99; Zara Picken pages 6, 122, 126; Gary Rose pages 39, 74, 80, 112; Ben Steers pages 23, 90, 98, 101, 120.